The Magic of Play

Jay Palmer

ISBN-13: 978-0-9911127-5-3

ISBN-10: 099111275X

*

All Books by Jay Palmer

The VIKINGS! Trilogy

- DeathQuest
- The Mourning Trail
- Quest for Valhalla

Jeremy Wrecker

Pirate of Land and Sea

The Magic of Play

Cover Artist: Piero Mng

DEDICATION

With eternal love,
to
Julitta of Rosehaven,
Where The Kittens Are,
Elysian Fields,
Heaven.

Chapter 1

Great Aunt Virginia

No one ever mentioned my Great Aunt Virginia, and whenever anyone accidentally dropped her name, angry hisses hushed everyone until all of us kids were rushed from the room. That's why I was amazed when, at the height of my parent's divorce, while they were screaming unspeakable things at each other, suddenly Mother packed my suitcase and Father drove me to the train station, hardly speaking a word. All the way to Baltimore I stared out of the window, listened to the monotonous rumble of the locomotive's great iron wheels, and sat beside a fat man reading a folded newspaper. What would my Great Aunt Virginia look like, and why was I, a twelve year old girl, left alone on a strange train, being sent to a woman that I knew nothing about?

My reflection in the dirty window belied my

worried expression. My bluebell-bright eyes darted nervously, my tight, frowning lips pursed and pouted, and my long brown hair hung in boring waves over my thin shoulders. I hated my dull hair-color except in bright sunlight when it shined like new chocolate.

"Baltimore!" the conductor finally announced.

Carrying my heavy suitcase, I was met on a crowded concrete platform by an austere, aged woman with bright silver hair like chrome wire spun about her head, each strand uniformly rigid and perfectly in place. She had sea-green eyes, was very thin, and wore a long, full dress; a tight bodice above ballooning skirts, under which only the toes of highly-polished, sharp-pointed shoes could be seen. Her dress appeared to be entirely of embroidered black silk with traces of white lace puffing out at her collar and cuffs. A broach on her collar showed a natural golden leaf trapped in a dark-glass oval, but it was of no plant that I recognized. She clutched a small black purse and a thick cane, upon which she leaned only lightly. The cane seemed to be made entirely of ebony, like the black keys on a piano, but it was smooth, intricately carved, and two small red gems gleamed from its handle like watchful eyes.

"You are my niece's daughter, Audrey Doris Virginia Darby," she said in a strict, crisp tone, with a certainty that surprised me, for never had we met. Nor had I closely equated my second middle name, which she stressed, with hers. I acknowledged her with an apprehensive nod. Why had I been sent to her? How long would I be here, and what would life be like with this strange old woman who looked like she'd just stepped out of a Dickens' novel?

Walking slowly beside her, I lugged my suitcase, containing my clothes, an extra pair of sneakers, and my laptop, which struck me as ironic; this old woman looked as if she'd never turned on a television, let alone a computer. I noticed that she didn't limp, and walked as if she didn't need her black cane.

As we reached the street, a great silver car, not a full limousine but very expensive, pulled up in front of us. A uniformed driver got out and opened the door for us, and Great Aunt Virginia ushered me inside. I swiftly reconsidered; life with this old woman might not be so bad if she was rich. In the car, she sat rigid with a taut frown and stared out of the tinted window; I silently wondered what her mansion would look like ... and if it had a pool. However, we drove to a very dilapidated section of town, and the driver let us out before a run-down, grubby tenement building, before which years of litter had collected on the sidewalk. Spray-painted gang-signs decorated its dirty concrete stairs; Great Aunt Virginia ignored them and directed me up the steps. Alarmed, I pulled hard on the rattling knob of a fingerprint-smeared glass-paned front door, but it held inviolate. A series of dirty white buttons beside a column of scrawled names showed that this was a secured entrance, not surprising in such a seedy section of town, but Great Aunt Virginia reached past me and opened the door as if no lock existed.

"Hurry, child; there's no time to lose," she said.

Ignoring the grimy elevator, Great Aunt Virginia led me up three flights of stairs, and we entered a small apartment which looked like an old movie set from the prehistoric black-and-white days. Faded wallpaper of dull-pinstripes covered the walls. Crystals hung from ancient lampshades, resembling tiny chandeliers, and dark-stained wooden chairs and couches bore affixed red velvet cushions. Bric-a-brac cluttered the apartment, and faded paintings of strange people, dressed in fashions not worn for a century, stared from wooden frames. Before the couch, rather than a coffee table, stood a short wooden table that seemed to be made for a small child of another age, and around it sat four tiny chairs. One chair was empty, but the other three held a red-plaid jacketed teddy bear with black-button eyes, a very old porcelain doll with long blonde hair wearing a flowing, lacey white dress, and a cloth-sewn jester doll, checkered red and black, all before a miniature pink and blue china tea set, carefully-arranged upon a spotless white lace tablecloth. I stared at the formal child's table and its doll occupants wondering if I'd fallen into a Norman Rockwell painting or if my Great Aunt Virginia was utterly mad.

"Leave your suitcase by the door," Great Aunt Virginia said, and she hurried me into her equally-antiquated kitchen. There she lit a wooden match and ignited an old gas stove, upon which she placed a large teapot whose distinctive markings matched the child's tea set in the living room. Then she turned to me. "Now, I know that you're not dressed properly, but that will have to wait. I don't suppose that you've ever made tea before?" She opened a great wooden cabinet that sat upon her kitchen counter; inside it were many tan-colored clay jars. "Take the stone pestle and ..."

"The ... the what?" I asked.

"This," she said irritably, and she tapped a thick, heavy green marble bowl that had a matching stone handle sticking out of it, which ended in a plain, rough, rounded bottom. "This is a mortar and pestle. You fill the pestle with tea leaves and then grind them with the mortar. Find the jar marked chamomile and take out two large sprigs."

"I ... I've never ...," I stammered.

"Obviously, but now you must," Great Aunt Virginia said. "Please hurry."

"Look, I don't know what's going on ..."

"Please!" she stressed, a desperate tone to her voice.

Worried, but fearing what might happen if I disobeyed, I sorted through the clay jars in the wooden cabinet and found one marked 'Chamomile', in which was a bunch of dried weeds. I took out two of the tiny branches, almost a third of her supply, and dropped them into the pestle.

"Chamomile is for calm, to steady us upon our journey," Great Aunt Virginia said. "Now add half a dandelion leaf."

I sorted through the jars again, worried that I might be expected to drink whatever I was mixing, until I found one marked 'Dandelion'. The dandelion leaf was long, dried, and brittle. I broke it in half and dropped one part into the mortar.

"Dandelion is for purity, for only the pure may cross the great river. Next, add three berries of sumach, for we need to arrive whole and in good health."

"I really don't like tea," I said.

"Nonsense," Great Aunt Virginia scoffed. "How can you not like what you've never tried? Add the sumach berries first, and then add five blossoms of sweet balm."

Nine different herbs and spices I added as she closely supervised, and then I ground them into fine powder with the mortar. The pungent aroma tickled my nose and made me feel heady, but I ground until the ancient kettle began to whistle and she turned off the stove.

"You know ... they sell tea bags in grocery stores," I said.

"We need homemade; that's very important," Great Aunt Virginia said. "There are many different recipes, too, each of which has a slightly different effect or takes you to a different place."

"Place? How can ...?"

"Mind your grinding, child. Every leaf and twig must be finely crushed."

Soon she pronounced my grinding 'Satisfactory', although with a disdainful sniff that left an exasperated expression on her finely-lined face. She took the lid off her steaming kettle and then had me hold my palms together as she spooned the powdery mess into my bare hands.

"Now, gently breathe upon it, and then cast it into the water."

"Breathe on it?"

"Do it."

I couldn't stay. I needed to call home, to tell my parents how insane Great Aunt Virginia was. Surely they'd come and rescue me. But I hadn't seen a phone, and doubted if one existed in this bizarre museum. If only mom had given me the cell phone that I'd wanted for Christmas ...!

With no recourse, I placated my great aunt. I lightly exhaled upon the dry powder, and then dropped the whole mess into the steamy kettle. Its strong scents instantly filled the kitchen with a fragrant, floral, invigorating tanginess that swelled my senses and made me deeply inhale.

"The tea has to steep," Great Aunt Virginia said. "Let's wait in the parlor."

Carrying the hot teapot with a potholder to the tiny doll's table, we sat side-by-side on the antique couch, whose red velvet cushions were hard and uncomfortable, not deep and soft. She opened an old wooden box which began to tinkle a slow, merry tune.

"I know this must seem improper," Great Aunt Virginia said, "but time presses and all explanations would utterly fail to impress the severity of our situation. Trust me, my dear Audrey: you'll soon understand everything."

"What's going on?" I asked. "What's so urgent?"

"My friends are in danger," Great Aunt Virginia said, a bitter regret filling her voice. "My friends need help, and I'm too old."

"Friends?" I asked.

She glanced longingly at the three dolls sitting in the chairs before her make-believe tea set, and I covered my mouth with my hand, fearing that I'd scream. What were they thinking, sending me here? This batty old woman should be locked up! I may only be twelve, but I'd won three times at Battle of Arcinthia and I could beat any of my classmates at War-Driver. I liked electronic toys, fast food, and modern music, not hot tea, ancient dolls, and wind-up music boxes.

We sat in silence for five minutes, and then her insanity proved itself.

"Pour for all five of us, please," Great Aunt Virginia said.

I glanced disbelieving; *five?* It was one thing for an old woman to display treasures from her childhood; quite another to believe that they were real. Fear clenched my spine, but what could I do? I considered running out of the door, but in this neighborhood, was that any safer than drinking tea with a mad woman?

Best to play along, I decided, and then to phone mother, so I poured some of the steaming tea into the large cup which Great Aunt Virginia held out to me, then into each of the four small cups on the table, one in front of each of the three dolls and one before the empty chair.

"Now sit at the table."

"I ... I'd rather not," I said, looking at the little baby-chair.

"You must," Great Aunt Virginia insisted. "These are your friends, too, and you don't want to start by offending them."

Offend? Children's toys? Surely she couldn't expect ...!

"I'd like to call home," I said.

"Later. First, we sit and drink."

"I don't like tea."

"Sit."

Only her stern manner made me obey, but my rebellious side was rising; soon I'd display a tantrum seldom seen by adults. Huffily I squeezed onto the hard wooden seat, my hips tightly wedged between the tiny chair's arms. I glanced at each of the three infantile doll's faces, feeling only contempt for their old-world ludicrousness.

Great Aunt Virginia leaned over and placed a

strange, powdery-brown straw into each tea cup on the table.

"This is a cinnamon stick. Use it like a spoon to stir your tea clockwise three times."

She put a cinnamon stick into her own glass, and then carefully stirred her tea clockwise three times, counting aloud as she did. Alarmed, but seeing no harm in it, I followed her example, watching the tiny floating herbs swirl in my cup.

"Drink."

Warily I lifted the steaming cup to my lips. Its spicy aroma filled my nostrils; it actually smelled good. I risked a tiny sip. It was bitter; I preferred soda.

"Just a little more; we won't be going for long."

Feeling utterly foolish, I took another sip. What my schoolmates would say if they saw me doing this I shuddered to think about. I'd be a laughingstock if a .jpg ever circulated of me having tea with three ridiculous dolls.

Suddenly my vision blurred ... and then cleared again. My thoughts grew fuzzy and my head started to spin.

"What ... what's going on?" I demanded, alarm raising my voice, my patience lost. "What have you given me?"

"Patience, dear Audrey," Great Aunt Virginia said. "Look at your friends; they're enjoying their tea."

The three dolls sat unmoving in their chairs, yet as my panic grew, they seemed harmless no longer, now inanimate threats from some spooky Twilight Zone episode, stark and silent, dangerous beyond their innocent countenances. My heart beat fast, my breath rapid; *what were all those herbs that I'd drunk?* What was in them? Were they something other than what Great Aunt Virginia had named? Was this even my real aunt? I'd never seen her before, not even a picture; this could be some insane stranger impersonating her. Why was I playing with a child's tea set like some brainless kindergartener?

Suddenly I heard voices laughing, one deep and harsh, another high and whiney, the third soft and musical. I felt very dizzy, my head spun, and I was certain that I was going to be sick. Bright light cascaded upon me, and I winced under its glare.

"Welcome!" said the soft, musical voice. "So ... you are Great Niece Audrey!"

Blindness replaced my dizziness; the sun was in my eyes, streaming in through the window; no, it was beaming directly upon my face. A strong breath of wind blew through my hair, suffusing a feeling of expansive openness incongruent with apartment walls: I was outdoors ... in a wide, grassy field filled with bright yellow flowers. The tea cup in my hand was large, not tiny, but otherwise identical, with exactly the same pink and blue floral pattern. The wooden table before me was high and thick under its white lace tablecloth, set exactly as the miniature tea set had been, but with adult-sized plates, cups, and saucers. My chair was suddenly twice as wide as I, and my feet hung a foot above the soil beneath me, my toes just brushing the tips of the tall grasses and flowers.

Three strange people sat before me, each resembling the dolls that had sat in their places. The teddy bear was a huge man with coarse black hair grown thick on his head, face, chest, and arms, and only his jovial smile, and that he and Great Aunt Virginia were hugging tightly, delayed my screams. He was wearing a thick red plaid jacket, rolled up at the sleeves, with no shirt, just like the teddy bear had worn. Great Aunt Virginia went from him to the jester, a thin, wiry young man, with a crooked smile, who wore a colorful outfit of red and black squares, which decorated even his comical cap with its three tiny bells. He hugged Great Aunt Virginia, and as he did, his sly fingers tickled her waist, and to my utter astonishment, rather than slap him, Great Aunt Virginia giggled like a coy schoolgirl and playfully batted flat the plush top of his tri-pointed cap. Then she went to the last person at the table, who slowly stood to embrace her. This young woman was beautiful, her skin perfect and features flawless, slender and graceful from her long blonde hair to the hem of what looked like a stunning wedding dress. I stared at her; no runway supermodel on the cover of any magazine ever matched her beauty.

"What's happened?" Great Aunt Virginia asked them.

"Terrible warnings," the tall, bear-like man said. "The infants are still missing, and ..."

"Now is not the time for sad news," the beautiful blonde said, and she turned to face me. "Our new friend has joined us at last!"

"Indeed, we must greet to our new savior!" the jester said, and suddenly, with amazing dexterity, he jumped up onto the table, swept off his colorful tinkling cap, and bowed low to me. Likewise, the big hairy man in the red plaid jacket fumbled to stand and deeply bow, and the beautiful blonde bride performed a perfect curtsey.

I screamed at last, pressing back against my chair, pushing hard on its sturdy wooden arms in utter horror. My shrill screech strained my voice until I thought I'd tear my vocal cords, and I blasted the whole flowery clearing, echoing deep into the thick, threatening woods surrounding us. Great Aunt Virginia and the three strangers froze and stared, appalled, and when the bride took a hesitant step toward me, Great Aunt Virginia stayed her with a soft hand. I screamed until my lungs emptied, and then gasped several deep, panting breaths.

"Are you quite finished?" Great Aunt Virginia asked. "There's no need for ill-behavior."

"Where am I? What did you give me? What was in that tea?"

"You mixed and ground it," Great Aunt Virginia reminded me. "My tea set brought you here, not the tea."

"W-what?"

"Tea isn't required," Great Aunt Virginia explained. "Good tea makes every journey easier, but I've come here many times without it."

"Where's ... here?"

"Explanations must wait," Great Aunt Virginia said. "We must help Falcon."

Falcon? I had no idea what they were talking about, but the tall bride slid gracefully forward and held out her delicate hand. Hesitantly I touched her slender fingers; she was real, warm and solid, and she gently drew me from my chair and led me toward the nearby dark woods, all the while smiling at me.

"Where are we going?" I asked.

"To save our friend," she replied.

Under the deep shadows of the trees, the sunlight of the clearing behind us shone far brighter than the dim rays filtering through the thick, leafy ceiling. Knotted, gray-black trunks leered, gnarled and wrinkled; I didn't like this forest. Inches from our path on each side lay broken, fallen branches, tall weeds, and the white points of countless sharp thorns threateningly stretching out from wicked, curling vines. In a small open space, illuminated by a wide ray of sunlight, I spied an awful sight: a tall, thin man covered in blood, his ragged clothing falling off of him, revealing skin covered with countless tiny cuts, but the man was bleeding no longer. He stood unmoving with an agonized stare in his frozen eyes, his mouth open in a silent scream, trapped inside a giant crystal of what looked like pure glass.

"Audrey, this is Falcon," Great Aunt Virginia said. "Don't be afraid; Falcon's still alive, but only barely. He'll die soon ... if he's not healed."

"How can he be ...?" Alive, I wanted to say, but the word caught in my throat. *This man was encased in glass, unable to breathe ...!*

"I put him in there," the bride said. "It was the only way to keep him alive until you arrived."

"Here," said the thin, little man in the bizarre jester's costume, and he handed me ... of all things ... an old green plaited jump rope.

I examined the jump rope in my hand: a plain braided cord, faded green, between two worn wooden handles. Confused, I stared at them.

"Just do as I say ...," Great Aunt Virginia said.

"I'm through listening!" I shouted, unable to restrain myself any longer. *"I've been doing what you said, and ... and ...!"*

"A man's life depends on you," the large, bearish man said, his voice very deep and serious.

My tantrum was about to explode. I wanted to throw the jump rope at them and run away, but *... how could a man's life depend on me?*

"Just repeat after me," Great Aunt Virginia said, and suddenly she started to chant a jump rope song.

"Two steps, four steps,
Six steps, eight

Around and round the holy tree
Over the mandrake
Little boys run and shout
Little girls squeal
Blessed be the holy tree
Forth the magic heal!"

Great Aunt Virginia repeated this over and over, gesturing for me to recite with her. The others stared at me with grim expectation. I could jump rope blindfolded, so I repeated her song; the rhyme was easy, simplistic, yet I was terribly afraid. My questions seemed too implausible to ask, as if their utterance would verify this madness.

"Keep going," the bride urged, pulling Great Aunt Virginia and the men back. "Keep chanting ... and start jumping rope."

These people were utterly mad, I knew, but I had no idea where I was, and until I could find a police officer, there was little that I could do. I'd learned to jump rope when I was four, and no harm had ever come from it, so I complied. Easily I flipped the rope over my head and jumped over it as it slapped the ground while I sang their childish song. I did a basic Double Bounce, the simplest and easiest style of jump roping. Their eyes watched me intently and then shifted to Falcon, frozen in his solid glass crystal.

A strange feeling washed over me. My plain jump rope seemed to sparkle, to shine in the dark forest, as if the old green cord had a light of its own. The gold and silver flashes illuminated everything, banishing the malevolent shadows. A strange sound, like a high-pitched singing, or many violins, filled the air as I watched the green cord flip over my head and fly down to slap the ground. Then, as I chanted, a change came over Falcon; very slowly, almost imperceptibly: the blood covering him started to vanish. The thousand tiny cuts slowly closed, as if healing in seconds what should've taken weeks, but not smoothly; in spurts, with each slap of my rope and the rhythm of my song. Then I realized it: each time that my sparkling jump rope passed over my eyes ... Falcon healed a little more.

Amazed, I kept jumping rope and chanting the song.

Finally his ragged garments began mending themselves ... until his shredded rags became an old-fashioned brown leisure suit over a white turtleneck shirt, all looking brand new. The music grew very loud and a weariness that I couldn't explain struck me. I stumbled; the rope slapped into my ankles and I almost fell.

"Princess Gracely, hurry!" the hairy man said.

The bride reached out and touched the great glass crystal encasing the living man. Instantly it began to shrink, melting, vanishing as if it had never existed. The tall, thin man inside it gasped and coughed, staggering as if too ill to stand. He had a large beak of a nose and a very tired expression, and held a hand to his head as if pained and weary.

"Thank you, Audrey," the bride said in her sweet, soft voice, but my eyes blurred. I felt dizzy, weakened by my jump roping, and feared that I'd fall.

"Come back soon!" the jester shouted, but his voice seemed to echo from far away.

Chapter 2

Doubting My Sanity

The arms of the tiny chair squeezed against my hips like a wooden vise. I opened my eyes; a stuffed teddy bear, a porcelain bride, and a cloth jester doll stared silently back at me across a child's tea set. I glanced at the couch; Great Aunt Virginia sat very still, her no-longer-steaming tea cup tightly clutched, her eyes closed. Slowly she seemed to awaken.

"Bless you, Audrey; you saved Falcon."

I stared at her.

"That ... that couldn't have ...!"

"Acceptance comes with time," Great Aunt Virginia said as she wearily opened her eyes. "Come, I'll show you to your room."

"But ...!"

"We'll discuss it later."

From a small, dark, door-filled hallway, a creaky wooden door opened upon a tiny room crammed with a narrow bed covered in stuffed animals. Framed pictures of horses decorated its faded lily-wallpaper. A chest of drawers stood shoved in one corner and an old steel radiator sat under its only narrow window, which was heavily-curtained. No closet door showed. Frowning, I set my suitcase on the bed; my room at home was twice this size and had a TV.

"Unpack."

"Where were we ...?"

"It's called Arcadia."

Great Aunt Virginia closed my door, leaving me alone. I stared at the strange room, wondering what child had last slept here, and if the room had even been occupied in my lifetime. But I couldn't wait any longer; I flipped open my suitcase and pulled out my laptop. Impatiently I waited through the restart, and then clicked to log online. If no signal was in range, then I was dead.

My default webpage loaded like a lifeline from Heaven. I clicked to my email, ignored the announcement that I had mail, and opened a blank message. I selected all of Mother and Father's email addresses, and in the subject line, I typed:

'HELP! COME GET ME!!!'

I tabbed to the body, but my fingers froze over the keys. What could I say? Had it been a dream? A hallucination? Had Great Aunt Virginia drugged me? It'd seemed so real! What could I tell Mother and Father?

I glanced at the many plastic eyes staring deathly

back at me from all of the stuffed animals, and suddenly I felt exposed. I left the body of my email blank and clicked 'Send'. Then I closed and hid my computer under the bed; what would Great Aunt Virginia do if she discovered it? *Would she even know what email was?*

Worried, after examining every crevice of my tiny room, I sat for an hour. My window was nailed shut, which was illegal and dangerous in case of fire. Its only view fell straight down to a filthy alley, and it looked across at one closed, shuttered window in an otherwise featureless brick wall. The top two shelves of the chest of drawers were empty, the third full of old sweaters, and the bottom drawer held a single folder quilt which filled it entirely. Uneasily I waited, trying not to look at the eyes of the many stuffed animals, until a hand knocked softly upon my door.

Great Aunt Virginia led me back to her kitchen, where she sat me at a small table with another white lace tablecloth and a single rose in a silver bud vase. On the wall over the table hung an antique board of many pegs, seven across and nine down. Hanging on each wooden peg was a china tea cup, each unique and very beautiful. Their designs seemed to be from all over the world: Asian, African, Russian, even Mayan, which I only recognized from watching The Emperor's New Groove.

While I examined the exquisite antique tea cups, Great Aunt Virginia busied herself at the stove, stirring small and large pots, and masterfully flipping two pork chops in a skillet. Soon she brought two fancy china plates and set them on my table, and then she joined me. Besides the pork chops, which were covered top and bottom in a powdery mixture of herbs, lay baby asparagus and strange pale beans with dark spots, both vegetables liberally coated in a rich brown sauce.

"They're black-eyed peas cooked with bacon and molasses," Great Aunt Virginia explained, seeing my expression. "I shucked them just this morning."

The black-eyed peas tasted great, although I was certain that the rich sauce overwhelmed their simple, bland flavor. The pork chops were delicious.

"So, what did you think of Arcadia?" Great Aunt Virginia asked. "Have you convinced yourself that it was a dream?"

"That ... that couldn't ... have been real," I said hesitantly.

"Yes, you're too old to believe right away," Great Aunt Virginia said. "I tried to get your parents to let me take you years ago, when you were five, but they refused."

"Why ... why did ...?"

"I had no choice. It's wrong to use magic to compel others against their will, but look at me; I can't jump rope any longer. Without you, Falcon would've died."

"That ... that was ... real?"

"Most assuredly."

"But ... it can't be ... the real world ..."

"The world of science? I know what they teach in school these days, but there's more to life than what can be proven. The imagination is real. Love is real. The human spirit exists in realities far beyond the mere physical. Science is very real, and you should never stop studying it, but never think that man has discovered all that there is to know. Our universe is alive and growing; there're always new things to learn."

"Then why doesn't everybody know about Arcadia?"

"Because nobody believes children," Great Aunt Virginia said with a sigh. "By the time that people are old enough to examine the world with any authority, they've long stopped looking for worlds inside their hearts. Adults become as cold as their scales and microscopes. All humans have limits, Audrey; it's almost impossible for us to see anything that we don't believe in. The trick is to keep believing."

"But ... if that was real ... then how did I heal Falcon?"

"With your jump rope, of course."

"But I've used lots of jump ropes!"

"Yes, but did you ever believe? Did you know the proper chants? You will, my dear: I'll teach you everything."

I stared up at her, my half-eaten pork chop completely forgotten. This was too much: a fantasy world? Me ... *doing magic?* I had to be hallucinating. My friends would laugh if I made such wild claims. Yet Great Aunt Virginia looked the same as before, prim and proper, sitting at the table very stiffly, her back straight, her chrome-bright hair perfect, her expression both warm and stern.

"We'll go back soon," Great Aunt Virginia said. "It's important that you not be overwhelmed, or you'll become polluted with disbelief and never enter Acadia again. You need time to rest and recover before we return."

"What if ... what if I ... don't want to go back?" I asked.

"You must go back at least once," Great Aunt Virginia said. "Have you ever had someone do you a favor, someone that you wanted to thank, but never got to? Falcon is in your debt; you must return so that he may thank you properly. After that ... we shall see."

"Do ... do you have a phone?"

"No, but there's one nearby, and you can use it tomorrow."

We finished our dinner in silence. The glow of the curtained windows lessened; outside, the sun was setting. Great Aunt Virginia kept stealing piercing glances at me, but otherwise did nothing even remotely threatening. As we finished, I glanced around.

"Do you have a television?"

"Of course not: nasty, vile things."

"I watch it all the time."

"Programming young children; it ought to be illegal."

"It's not programming ..."

"Let's not discuss it. There are plenty of healthy distractions in my house, and you're free to explore. Now you must choose: you can explore my home seeking to prove that there's nothing here to interest you, in which case you'll be both successful and miserable, or you can look for new interests and experiences. The choice is yours."

"When will we be going back to ...?" I asked, unable to finish the question.

Great Aunt Virginia smiled.

"Tomorrow morning. Traveling is very taxing upon people my age; I want both of us to have a good night's sleep."

Great Aunt Virginia's house was cluttered with the oddest assortment of junk and old books that I'd ever seen. Little ceramic figures and ancient dolls of all shapes and sizes were everywhere, but not one spec of dust or dirt. Copies of Tom Sawyer and Huckleberry Finn were prominently displayed on one of her many bookshelves beside Charles Dickens' David Copperfield and Great Expectations, all very old, probably first editions, but in excellent condition. I was shocked to find some newer books on her shelf: the entire Redwall series, Elfquest graphic novels, and all seven Harry Potter books, the first two in strange, colorful editions that I'd never seen before. But they were far outnumbered by the long matching rows of Nancy Drew, the Hardy Boys, and ...

"The Wizard of Oz?" I asked, seeing the whole series. "I thought there was only one."

"Frank Balm penned fourteen Oz books before he died," Great Aunt Virginia said, sitting on the couch and flipping through a box of old photos. "It's a pity that they only made a movie of the first. Ah, here it is; come see."

Great Aunt Virginia showed me an old black and white photograph of a young girl, about eight, in a long skirt, holding the same jump rope that I'd used in Arcadia. She was very pretty and had extremely long hair, but the faded photo showed only indistinct features.

"That was me when I first learned to visit Arcadia," Great Aunt Virginia said with a smile.

"Very nice," I said.

As Great Aunt Virginia patiently stared at her photographs, I continued to look about the room at all of her strange antiques. I reached down and picked up the jester doll.

"Is this ... the little man in Arcadia?" I asked.

"His counterpart, you might call it," Great Aunt Virginia said. "That's just a doll; if you ripped it up – please don't – it would have absolutely no effect on Muskay. Yet there is a connection, a drawing, if you will, that pulls us together when we travel to his world."

"Muskay?"

"Muskay the Jester," Great Aunt Virginia smiled sweetly. "The bear is named Hiram, and the bride is Princess Gracely."

"But they aren't dolls in Arcadia ..."

"Dolls are never just dolls in the eyes of those who love them."

I scrutinized the well-sewn jester doll from every side, and then set it back in its chair. Next, I examined the fancy tea set. The child-sized dishes were obviously very old, but only because no one made such toys any more. Its condition was immaculate, not a chip or scratch marred its hand-painted ceramic surface. Beside the tea pot and cups were matching saucers, cake-plates, finger-bowls, spoon-rests, a tiny sugar bowl, a cream pitcher, a butter dish, three covered-bowls for jam, and several oval serving plates. A small bouquet of dried flowers with little yellow and purple buds sat in a matching flower vase. Tiny silver spoons, blunt, unsharpened knives, and three-pronged forks sat upon folded linen napkins, all with a formality to which only the Queen of England was accustomed.

I turned away so that Great Aunt Virginia couldn't see my face. I wasn't feeling threatened anymore, but I wanted to get back to my laptop; Mother and Father must've replied by now.

"I think I should go to bed," I said.

"As you wish," Great Aunt Virginia said, and

she set her box down. “Come.”

I was startled as she led me into the hall; there seemed to be more doors there now. I counted this time: five; one to my room, one to a small tiled bathroom, and three other doors, all closed. One of the doors she opened to reveal a large closet stuffed with junk to the ceiling, but nothing was piled in a disheveled or haphazard manner. Great Aunt Virginia opened a chest just inside of the door and lifted out a long silk nightgown of palest green.

“I have pajamas,” I said.

“A young lady should wear this.”

I took the nightgown rather than argue, and seconds later I was safely in my room.

“I'll be back to tuck you in,” Great Aunt Virginia spoke through the door.

Tuck me in? I was twelve, not six! Instantly I crawled under the bed to retrieve my laptop, yet my fingers closed on emptiness. I dropped down and looked about; nothing but carpet lay underneath the wooden slats of my bed: *Great Aunt Virginia had taken my computer!*

Consternation cascaded over me. Was she ever going to let me contact my family, or was she simply leading me on? Her fantasy-friend was healed; she didn't need me anymore. My temper was growing again, but I didn't dare confront her after dark in a strange town. Sighing, I put on the ridiculously-long nightgown and pulled my toothbrush out of my suitcase. Great

Aunt Virginia eyed me from the parlor as I crossed to the bathroom, but nodded approvingly when she spied my toothbrush. Then, as soon as I turned on my toothbrush, Great Aunt Virginia suddenly burst into the bathroom.

"What's that?" she cried.

I stood before the sink, my teeth slimed with toothpaste, staring up at her as if she were mad.

"It's a 'lectric toothb'ush," I mumbled.

"Electric ...?"

"It ... cleans teeth be''er."

"Better?" she looked shocked, but then her shoulders slumped and she frowned. "Well, if it's better ..."

Great Aunt Virginia watched as I finished brushing my teeth, her eyes fixed on my battery-powered travel toothbrush. I rinsed one last time, dried my hands and face, and then exited back to my room. She followed me into my bedroom and pulled back my covers as I set my toothbrush on the dresser. Warily I got into bed, watching her thinly-lined face and sea-green eyes, wondering where she'd hid my laptop. She pulled my covers up to my chin, and then sat down upon the bed beside me.

"Once upon a time ..."

"I'm not six!"

"Then you're old enough to judge the moral of my story," Great Aunt Virginia said, not even flinching as I frowned, sticking out my lower lip. She started her bedtime story again, ignoring my blatant displeasure.

"Once upon a time there were three beautiful girls. The first girl didn't believe in anything, not in magic or dreams, and she had a very nice, plain, dull life. The second girl believed in many dreams, big and small, and some of her dreams came true, but most didn't. She reveled in her dreams come true, but spent her days bitter and resentful for her dreams that never came to be. The third girl also believed in many dreams, and reveled in her few dreams that came true, but she only thought fondly of her dreams that never came to be, grateful for the momentary joys that her unfulfilled dreams had given her. The third girl was the happiest of all."

Great Aunt Virginia leaned over, kissed my forehead, and then left, closing my door behind her.

The next morning, I faced Great Aunt Virginia determinedly. Still in my borrowed nightgown, I found her in the kitchen, her chrome-wire hair as perfect as ever, again wearing black, but protecting her formal dress with a long white apron, washing dishes from her magic tea set in the sink.

"I want my laptop," I said firmly.

"I beg your pardon?" she asked. "Your ... *what?*"

"My laptop: my computer."

"You ... you brought a computer ... here?"

"Yes. I hid it under my bed, and now it's gone."

Great Aunt Virginia's slender eyebrows knitted and a deep frown thinned her lips.

"I don't know which is more reprehensible: the theft ... or the accusation," Great Aunt Virginia's voice strained, her words almost hissing. "Follow me."

She dried her hands on a towel and led me back into my bedroom, where my bed covers lay thrown back; I'd piled all of her stuffed animals on top of the chest of drawers. Great Aunt Virginia pulled my covers up and smoothed them, and then turned to face her stuffed animals.

"I'm ashamed of all of you," Great Aunt Virginia said to the dolls. "Whatever you've taken, please return it at once. Don't make me ask again."

Without another word, she ushered me out and closed my bedroom door.

"While we wait, you can get ready," Great Aunt Virginia said. "Take a bath. I left an appropriate garment for you hanging just inside of the bathroom door."

"What about my computer?" I asked.

"I'm sure that it will be returned."

Great Aunt Virginia turned huffily and walked back toward the kitchen. I stared at her; *she was utterly insane!* Did she think that this ruse would make me forget about my computer, or was she just trying to delay me again? I glanced at the front door, but I couldn't run outside wearing nothing but a silk nightgown, so I stomped into the bathroom and spun the faucets over the bathtub. Slowly the water grew hot, and soon a steaming tub stood waiting. I glanced across the tiny hall at my closed bedroom door; I'd kept the bathroom door open so that I could keep an eye on it. *Did she really expect ...?*

Irresistibly I stepped into the hall. Before I closed the bathroom door, I had to know: I grabbed the doorknob and twisted, then pushed open my bedroom door: on my bed covers, surrounded by all of the stuffed animals, clearly visible, lay my laptop.

I slammed my bedroom door, then fled into the bathroom and slammed its door behind me. *How could this be?* I'd watched that bedroom door like a hawk! Great Aunt Virginia couldn't have snuck past me. *Dolls can't move, steal laptops, and then return them!*

I stood alone, gasping, my heart hammering. I couldn't accept this! I didn't want to be one of those weirdo kids who had no friends and believed in childish impossibilities! Yesterday hadn't happened! I'd been dreaming ... having a nightmare! Yet the hard tile floor was cold beneath my feet, and the porcelain sink that I was clutching to keep from falling felt solid, and the bathwater was wafting inviting steam; this was real. *I was here.*

Knuckles rapped softly upon the door.

"Audrey, after you've bathed, will you try not to

slam my doors?"

I glanced at the door, and for the first time I saw the dress behind it; it was a hundred years old if it was a day. Its long skirt was dark green with a strange black vest that was laced up its front with white ribbons. *What was this, Halloween?* I couldn't go out in that!

My email, I thought; Mother and Father had to be almost here by now. My best bet was to keep playing along, but not to drink any more of Great Aunt Virginia's strange teas; if their effects were permanent then I could end up like her forever. I took my bath, put on the bizarre long dress, which was very restraining and uncomfortable, and opened the bathroom door. If only I could get to my laptop without ...

"Audrey! You look marvelous! Let me look at you," Great Aunt Virginia pulled me out into the parlor and made me turn around. "Finally: a young lady! Are you ready to go?"

"I need to check my computer."

"I'm sure that they didn't harm it."

"I'd like to check."

"If you must, but hurry; they're making our breakfast now and it'd be rude to arrive late."

I went back into my bedroom. Unfortunately, Great Aunt Virginia followed and stood impatiently in my doorway, waiting on me. Fearing to wait any longer, I opened my laptop and waited until I could log on to the closest unprotected site, then clicked 'Email'. Thirty-two messages were waiting, mostly from Mother. I opened the first.

'WHERE ARE YOU?'

That was all that the message said. I scrolled though several others, including one very long email professing her love for me and another begging whoever abducted me to release me. How could that be? They'd sent me here! They'd packed my suitcase and put me on the train! I hadn't bothered to mention where I was because ... *how could they not know?*

"What's the matter?" Great Aunt Virginia asked, and I realized how my expression must look.

"Nothing," I said quickly.

"Are you sending ... what's it called?"

I bit my tongue; *she knew!*

"Email," I confessed.

"To your parents?"

"Yes," I said, and I clutched my laptop protectively. If this old woman wanted a fight then she'd see what an angry young girl could do. *I wasn't going to surrender my laptop!*

"Be sure to give them my best," Great Aunt Virginia said, quite unperturbed. "Tell them that we're going out for breakfast, but that you will be calling them over the phone early this afternoon. Hurry; we're late."

Disbelieving, I stared at Great Aunt Virginia, then attacked my keyboard with my fingers, madly typing.

I'm at Great Aunt Virginia's. Come get me

ASAP!!!!! Hurry!!!!!!!

P.S. She says to say hi, and that we're going out to eat, but she'll let me call you this afternoon.

--Audrey

After sending, I closed my laptop and started to go out into the parlor, but then I stopped, turned around, and stared at the many stuffed animals beside my laptop; I'd been about to warn them not to steal my stuff again, but I caught myself in time. Shaking my head, I closed my door.

A war raged inside me; I should've told my parents what was going on, but part of me wanted no one to ever know.

"Come, sit down," Great Aunt Virginia said. "I'll pour."

The china tea set was all set out again and every dish shined, newly-washed and dried. Great Aunt Virginia stood beside the tiny table, the teapot in her hands.

"In your chair," Great Aunt Virginia directed.

"Can't I sit on the couch?"

"Next time; for now, without tea, you have to be fully immersed in every other way."

"No tea?"

"The magic's in the play, not the tea."

I squeezed myself into the tiny chair, facing the short, lace-covered table meticulously set with pink and blue tea cups, saucers, and all the other tiny dishes and silverware. Great Aunt Virginia smiled and then turned to the china bride-doll.

"Princess Gracely, you look remarkably lovely today!" Great Aunt Virginia leaned over and actually pretended to pour imaginary tea from the empty teapot into Princess Gracely's tiny cup. I stared at her; *how mad could you get?* "Muskay, you tease, may I serve?" She tipped the empty teapot, carefully holding the stem over his cup; nothing came out. "Why, thank you, but I'm sure there's a nicer way of saying good morning. Hiram, so nice to see you looking happy so early in the morning!" After pouring play-tea for all of them, Virginia turned and pretended to fill my cup. "Audrey, my favorite grand-niece, you look truly elegant in that dress. Would you like to keep it?"

She paused, staring at me as if expecting an answer.

"Ahhh, ummm ..., I ... really don't need it."

"Everyone needs to look elegant, especially pretty young women," Great Aunt Virginia said, and then she filled her own cup with imaginary tea. Finally she set the down empty teapot and lifted her cup. "Here's to you, Audrey, and your second visit to Arcadia." She stared hesitantly at me, then gestured to the tea cup in her hand. I stared, incredulous; *me? Drink imaginary tea? Was she senile?* Yet she gestured again, and I grimaced and picked up my empty tea cup. As Great Aunt Virginia did, I pretended to take a sip. "Audrey, dear, we don't have time for doubt and disbelief. Our breakfast is getting cold. Drink deep, and I'll never ask again. Believe!"

With a heavy sigh, I lifted my tiny tea cup again and drank the air inside it, remembering, almost missing, the taste of the spicy herb tea that I'd made yesterday. I glanced across the table at the red-plaid jacketed teddy bear, the cloth-sewn jester, and the painted china doll in her white-lace wedding dress, inanimate as always, their vacant eyes staring across the play tea set. I tilted back my cup and took a long, imaginary drink. This was silly, I kept thinking, feeling foolish, and then suddenly my vision blurred. I tried to peer through my suddenly-fuzzy sight ... and swore that I could see three dolls lifting tiny tea cups.

Chapter 3

Lessons Begin

"Three cheers for Audrey!" Falcon shouted.

"Three cheers!" a chorus of voices all around me repeated.

I startled; Great Aunt Virginia, Hiram, Muskay, and Princess Gracely were all before me, lifting their big tea cups and toasting me. I was again sitting at the great wooden table, the large pink and blue floral tea set carefully laid out before me, but no field of yellow flowers surrounded us.

Instead, surrounding us were four large, box-shaped, wooden horse-drawn carriages, minus the horses; their leather harnesses lay empty upon the ground. On the side facing the table, each boxy wooden cart had a huge, rectangular, heavily-decorated window draped with thick velvet curtains, drawn apart, each displaying a wide, miniature theatrical stage. Upon each stage hung dozens of stringed marionettes dancing in perfect synchronization, clapping their wooden hands and stomping their shiny boots. The marionettes were men and women, painted in matching blue and gold outfits with tall hats, each with a fluffy canary-yellow feather in front, and wearing gleaming black boots. Each appeared to be about fifteen inches tall, hanging from strings stretched to the ceilings of their four cart-borne stages, with bright-painted eyes of white half-spheres, dotted with brown-painted pupils, and glued to their polished natural-wood faces. In unison, their arms lifted, and their little black boots slammed down onto the wooden floors of their stages. They sang as they danced.

"Audrey! Audrey! Lover of dolls!
Welcome! Welcome! To our halls!
Magician! Healer! Maker of fate!
Praise her! Praise her! Audrey is great!"

For wooden puppets, they danced amazingly well. To my astonishment, as I ducked low, I spied their crossbraces, to which their strings were affixed, sliding over their heads against the ceilings of the wagon-stages, with no hands guiding them; these puppets were dancing on their own. But nothing rattled me anymore; magic simply existed in Arcadia. When they finished, with a great, boot-stomping flourish, I joined Great Aunt Virginia, Hiram, Muskay, and Princess Gracely in applauding. Then one marionette stepped forward and bowed, this one having a short, triangular, white-painted beard. To my amazement, he reached up, gathered his strings, and pulled hard; his wooden crossbrace fell, and he caught it, spun it a few times to bind up most of his strings, and then slung it over one shoulder like a backpack. Then he jumped off of the stage and landed right onto our big table while we were still applauding.

"Princess Audrey, welcome to Theater City, home of the marionettes," he said loudly, as if reciting a rehearsed speech, and then he bowed low again.

"Princess ...?" I asked.

"As your wonderful great aunt before you," the marionette said, turning and bowing to Great Aunt Virginia.

"Master Strand, we thank you deeply," Great Aunt Virginia said, and she held her tea cup aside and bowed slightly, as if curtseying in her chair. He bowed again.

"Master Strand manages the marionettes," Princess Gracely explained in her soft, sweet voice. "They begged us to be the first to welcome you to Arcadia."

"Our humble service to she who will save us!" Master Strand said with a bow to Princess Gracely.

"Save ...?" I asked.

"Now isn't the time," Hiram's deep, bear-like voice growled.

"Indeed!" Muskay sat up with a laugh. "Now is the time for sweets!"

"Ta-da!" Falcon sang out, and he appeared

from behind one of the stage-carts with a wide, low cake covered in brightly-lit candles. He carried the flaming, round cake to the table and set it before me. "To Princess Audrey, for her heroic saving of my most unworthy, but very important to me, life."

With a smile, Falcon lifted a long, sharp cake knife, but then stood aside expectantly. The candles on the cake spelled 'Audrey'. I smiled shyly and tried to make a wish, but I couldn't decide if I wanted to wish Arcadia real or not. Easily I blew out all of the candles in one breath, and everyone cheered again.

"Thank you all," I said politely as Falcon cut the cake.

He served me first, then Great Aunt Virginia, Princess Gracely, and then Hiram and Muskay. The cake wasn't like a birthday cake, layered in frosting, but a sweet cornbread with an orange-glaze and small black seeds, which I didn't recognize but were very tasty, and more-appropriate for breakfast than cake. I quickly ate several bites; it was hot, moist, and delicious. I complimented Falcon several times.

"Thank you," he chimed repeatedly. "It's the least that I could do."

"How did you get all those cuts?" I asked.

"Audrey, not during breakfast!" Great Aunt Virginia scolded.

"She has a right to know," Hiram said, lifting another slice of cake, and he nodded to Falcon. "Tell her."

"Well, I can't really say," Falcon said. "That is, I never saw what attacked me. I don't normally do dangerous assignments; I prefer to sit back and mumble dire predictions. That was why I agreed to go; the disappearances were over, so the site should've been empty."

"Disappearances?" I asked.

"It has happened three times," Hiram said. "Then an ordinance of tin soldiers on a routine scouting mission failed to return."

"Tin soldiers?"

"Our very best fighters ... gone without a trace," Muskay said. "Very suspicious."

"I went alone, as they'd vanished a week before," Falcon said. "I searched all day without finding anything but the tin soldier's tracks, which I followed until sunset. The full moon was shining bright, so I kept searching the woods by the river late into the night. Then, suddenly, I heard a strange humming sound, and a great shadow blocked out the moon. I was trapped in darkness, unable to see my hand in front of my face, while the humming grew louder and closer. I tried to run, but in the darkness, I kept stumbling into trees. Blind, I had to follow the trail bent low, by feel alone. The source of the humming grew deafening; I cried out, but no one was near. Then I felt the first cut, and soon tiny, sharp claws were slicing me apart from every side."

"Claws …?"

"I assume so; I couldn't see anything. All that I heard was a loud humming, and all that I felt were slashes shredding my clothes and my flesh. Protecting my eyes, I ran screaming into one tree after another, stumbling over underbrush, until I tripped and fell headfirst into the river."

"He was lucky," Muskay sneered. "No one else has survived the Death of a Thousand Cuts."

"Death of a Thousand Cuts …?"

"That's what we call it," Hiram said. "Others have been found sliced to ribbons, lost beyond all hope."

"It's some great, new menace," Master Strand said, nodding grimly. "We've spoken to the Lonely Wanderers; they suspect that some terrible new monster has appeared, something with a hundred arms, each with a razor-sharp claw."

"That's just speculation," Princess Gracely said.

"What else could cause such injuries?" Master Strand asked.

"What are Lonely Wanderers?" I asked.

"Lonely Wanderers are our revered ancestors," Princess Gracely said.

"There are few left," Master Strand said. "Dolls who haven't had loving owners in an eon; some have counterparts in museums; others lie in archeological sites yet to be discovered."

"Simple clay figures, most of them," Muskey said derisively. "Can't move their arms or legs; have to hop all over. Some are finger puppets."

"Poor, desolate souls," Great Aunt Virginia said. "They are the forgotten dolls, the most ancient of us all."

"We need to go back to that site," Hiram said.

"Not me!" Falcon said.

"We must examine where you were attacked and look for clues," Princess Gracely said. "If there's a new threat to Arcadia ..."

"Then you can show us where they are!" Muskay gave Falcon a broad, leering smile.

"I almost died!" Falcon argued.

"You won't be alone this time," Princess Gracely said.

"With all of us, you'll be safe enough," Hiram added.

"You don't know what it's like," Falcon said. "Even with your magic ..."

"Can I come?" I asked.

Everyone paused and turned to look at me.

"We could use a jumper," Hiram said.

"She's not ready!" Great Aunt Virginia insisted.

"She might be all that can save us," Princess Gracely said. "Human magic is far superior to doll magic."

"Yes; what a pity!" Muskay scowled.

"We don't know what we're facing," Great Aunt Virginia pointed out.

"That's why we must go," Hiram said. "If we

don't uncover the threat, then soon it may be too late."

"Wouldn't it be good practice for her?" Muskay asked. "Audrey looks pretty bright; she picked up the healing spell fast enough, and I'd rather take a jumper along."

"She's not prepared for a long fight," Great Aunt Virginia said.

"I'm not afraid," I said.

"It's not a question of courage," Great Aunt Virginia began.

"Speak for yourself," Falcon interrupted.

"Please, I want to help," I said to Great Aunt Virginia. "You told me that these people are our friends …"

Great Aunt Virginia looked doubtful, but finally she resigned.

"You'll have to start practicing right now," Great Aunt Virginia said. "Arcadia may seem like a fantasy, but death here is very real."

Grimly I nodded. Great Aunt Virginia stared unhappily, and then slowly lifted her hand. Upon her outstretched palm hung the green jump rope that I'd used to heal Falcon.

Many of Master Strand's fellow marionettes came over to watch as Great Aunt Virginia started teaching me a new charm, each with their strings gathered as best they could, their crossbraces over one shoulder. I smiled at them and easily jumped the rope, still using only basic

Double Bounces as I sang.

"Shield, shield, never yield
Strengthen now your mighty field
Grow tight! Grow bright!
Make your magic now congeal!
My shelter now erect!
Our defense now bedeck!
Hard! Strong! Last long!
Let your safeguard us protect!"

As always, the chant was simple, giving me time to examine Theater City. Each carriage held a tiny stage, some with their rich velvet curtains closed, others wide open. None seemed to have any furniture; some marionettes were resting in sitting positions, their strings holding them up as if they were relaxing on comfortable loungers, others practicing dancing in unison, stopping often to correct one dancer or demonstrate a difficult move. Master Strand stayed standing on our table in deep discussion with Hiram and Princess Gracely, and all three occasionally glanced at me. Falcon seemed to be walking back and forth across the small city of tiny theaters as if trying to escape Muskay, who kept following him, asking questions like 'What if they come here?' and 'How many cuts do you think that you could survive?'.

"Concentrate," Great Aunt Virginia instructed me. "Focus on the words."

I chanted as forcefully as I could, though not

knowing why, when suddenly my jump rope began to shine again, and each loop over my head traced a thin, sparkling field behind it.

"That's it," Great Aunt Virginia said. "Concentrate harder."

I clenched my teeth and concentrated. Slowly the glow increased and the sparkles grew denser, but it was hard to focus, like concentrating on a math test with firecrackers exploding all around. Clearly I could see the strength of my field increase as I concentrated, yet suddenly I felt drained, as if my focus, generating the magic, sapped my strength. I redoubled my effort, encouraged by the cheers and applause of the watching marionettes, and soon the glittering sphere of my jump rope grew almost solid, as if I were jumping inside a glowing globe of gold and silver sparkles.

"Keep focusing," Great Aunt Virginia called from outside my sphere. "You're almost there."

Almost? I gritted my teeth and concentrated, despite my growing exhaustion. Slowly the glowing sphere around me grew, stretching out beyond the radius of my jump rope. It expanded wider and higher, making a bright circle upon the ground around me. It passed through Great Aunt Virginia until she and half of the marionettes stood inside my shield.

"That's it, Audrey!" Great Aunt Virginia shouted. "Keep going!"

I couldn't. The strain grew ... and my energy failed. My rope faltered; I missed a jump and lost momentum.

The shining, shimmering gold and silver shield faded, and vanished a moment later. The marionettes stopped cheering, and Great Aunt Virginia frowned.

"Why ... why is this so ... hard?" I asked.

"Magic costs," Great Aunt Virginia said. "You need a break. Gentlemen, ladies; Audrey needs to rest."

Reluctantly, all of the marionettes bowed and quickly walked away.

"I ... don't understand," I said. "They're dolls, and they look like dolls, but Hiram, Muskay, and ..."

"... and Princess Gracely look like people," Great Aunt Virginia said, lowering her voice. "How many of your friends play with marionettes?"

"None."

"Exactly: their counterparts in our world are unloved. No one owns them, talks to them, or cares about them. They're not special to anyone, so they're just dolls, especially here."

"But ... you're not the only one with dolls!"

"Of course not, but Arcadia isn't the only kingdom here; many exist. All of these people ... they're people no matter what form they take ... have counterparts in our world. This land is like a dimension of our own world; it's still Earth, with tall mountains and vast oceans. There have always been fewer dolls than people, and dolls are smaller.

They live spread out. Take Falcon; he's someone else's doll, a Boston family heirloom, I believe, always passed to each youngest child, and his counterpart has more patches than original fabric. But he's one of the lucky; most of these toys have been abandoned and unloved for years, even centuries."

"That's sad."

"Hiram, Muskay, and Princess Gracely are mine, and I love them very much," Great Aunt Virginia said. "Someday ... I hope to leave them to you."

I glanced at her, surprised and frightened. I couldn't refuse, but besides the responsibility, did I really want to become like Great Aunt Virginia?

"We don't have much time," Great Aunt Virginia said. "For now, there's another rhyme that you must learn:

Red rope, white rope, blue rope twirled
Every curve's a straight line
Every straight line's curled
Past oceans and mountains
Each flag unfurled
Hop around! Hop around!
Hop around the world!
Carry me, carry me!
Carry me alone!
Carry me, carry me
To Aunt Virginia's home!"

"Will that take me to your house?" I asked.

"Yes, ... from anywhere in the world. Never forget

it, for from now on ...," Great Aunt Virginia took the jump rope from my hands, coiled it, and looped it over my head and one arm so that it hung from my shoulder to hip. "From now on, this is your jump rope: Audrey, you are a jumper."

I smiled widely.

"Don't thank me yet," Great Aunt Virginia said. "See all of these poor, helpless, innocent dolls and puppets? You're their magician now; their only hope in a darkening world."

"What? I ... never ...!"

"Who else? I can't jump rope anymore; I have trouble walking up steps. The greatest responsibility of a protector is to see to it that their charges remain protected, even if they themselves fall. Like it or not, old age is defeating me, and all my magic can't overturn nature for long. If you don't take it, then, despite five decades of protecting, I'll have failed."

I stared at her, and slowly my eyes unexpectedly blurred.

"Time to go home," Great Aunt Virginia sighed.

Chapter 4

Troubled Reality

"Open this door!" Mother's voice screamed as fists pounded on the front door. "Audrey!"

I opened my eyes to Great Aunt Virginia's apartment.

"Perhaps you should open the door," Great Aunt Virginia said calmly. "I'll make some tea."

As fists banged, I unlocked and opened the front door, and Mother, nearly-hysterical, burst inside and seized me tightly.

"My baby! My baby!"

"That's her, officer," Father said.

A tall, frowning police officer peeked around Father from the hallway.

"Welcome, Charlotte and Jack," Great Aunt Virginia smiled from the kitchen. "Please come in. I'm making tea."

"Hold on," the police officer said, stepping in front of Father and looking down at me. He glanced at a tiny notebook in his hand. "Are you Audrey Doris Virginia Darby?"

"Yes, sir."

"Have you been abducted?"

"Abducted ...?"

"How did you get to Baltimore?"

"Father put me on a train."

Mother's head jerked to stare at Father, and the policeman's eyes slowly followed hers.

"Jack!" Mother shouted.

"I didn't ...!" Father insisted.

"Sir, do you know the penalty for falsely reporting a crime?"

"Sir, I assure you ...!"

"Officer, if I may?" Great Aunt Virginia interrupted. "Charlotte is my niece. Her husband Jack has had ... well, problems like this before: memory issues."

"I have not!" Father bellowed.

"Father, you keep every receipt," I said. "If you put me on a train ..."

"That's right! Hold on," Father pulled out his wallet, opened it, and fumbled through a small stack of thin, printed receipts. He shuffled through them, then froze, his face paling. *"It ... it can't be ...!"*

"May I see that?" The officer took the receipt and examined it. "A receipt from a train station; are these the last four digits of your credit card number?"

"Yes, but ... I swear ... I didn't ... I don't remember ...!"

"We're very sorry for wasting your time, officer," Great Aunt Virginia said.

The officer stared at each of them very coldly, then handed Father his receipt.

"If it happens again, you'll explain it to a judge."

"Y-y-yes, officer," Father stammered, still staring uncomprehendingly at the receipt.

The police officer walked back to the elevator.

"Jack, how could you ...?"

"I didn't ... I don't know how ...!"

"No point worrying about it now," Great Aunt Virginia said. "It's been ... what, eleven years since we last saw each other? Please come in. Make yourselves at home. Audrey, invite them properly. The tea is steeping."

Great Aunt Virginia disappeared into the kitchen and I untangled myself from Mother's arms.

"Please come in," I said, and, seeing their shocked expressions, I added, "Really; I'm fine."

"Where did you get that dress, and what's this?" Mother asked, fingering the green coil over my shoulder.

"Great Aunt Virginia gave ... I mean, lent me this dress, and this is a jump rope."

"A jump rope?" Father snorted. "We're up all night, frantic, wondering where you are ... what happened to you ...!"

Father stepped forward as Mother gave him room to enter, and he bent and hugged me stiffly, the mysterious train receipt now worriedly pinched between two his fingers as if it were a deadly black widow spider. I hugged him back, then closed the front door, and drew him and Mother into the parlor.

"Are you sure ... you're alright?" Mother asked.

"Yes, we just ate ... well, we just got back from eating, and then you knocked."

Mother and Father exchanged confused glances, but Mother shook her head slightly and Father's frown deepened.

"Are you ready to go?" Father asked.

"No, ... I mean, I have to change first."

"Well, go change," Father said. "It's a long drive back."

I nodded and went to my room. My laptop was still on my bed, but my bed was now newly-made, my covers perfectly smooth and flat, and the stuffed animals now lay in a strange arrangement from my pillow to the foot of my bed. It took a second for me to realize that, from the positions of their bodies, they spelled out the word 'Sorry'.

"I forgive you," I smiled at them. "I hope that I'll see you again soon."

Seconds later, I stood in my jeans again, enjoying the comfortable feel of my cotton T-shirt. I left the dress neatly folded on my bed beside the jump rope, stuffed my laptop and toothbrush into my suitcase, and hurried out.

"Still playing with dolls," Father scowled as Great

Aunt Virginia came out of the kitchen with a tray of tea cups. Father was still standing by the door, but Mother was on her knees before the magic tea set.

"This is incredible," Mother said. "Great Grandma Annie had this table set up in her living room, exactly like this; it's one of the few memories that I have of her."

"She was an amazing, strong, and wise woman," Great Aunt Virginia said, and she glanced at me. "She was my great aunt."

Father's frown reached monumental proportions.

"We should go ...," he said.

"Your first visit to my house ... and you can't stay ten minutes?" Great Aunt Virginia asked coldly. "At least have some tea before you go; it'll calm you."

I smiled; if Great Aunt Virginia had said that her tea would turn Father into an elephant then I wouldn't disbelieve her for a second. Father hesitated, then stepped forward and took a saucer and tea cup from her tray. Mother reached up and took a cup, but examined it suspiciously, unlike Father, who drank his at once.

"Audrey, did you pack your jump rope?" Great Aunt Virginia asked.

"No, I ..."

"You'd best go get it," Great Aunt Virginia lowered her brows and gave me a meaningful stare.

"It's your jump rope now, and you should always keep it with you."

By the time that I returned, the magic jump rope stuffed into my suitcase, Mother was describing her last contacts with half of our family. Father scowled when she mentioned his three brothers, all of whom he avoided whenever he could, but he did speak a few nice words about Aunt Muriel's wedding, especially about the open bar. However, soon the tea cups were empty, Father fidgeting and Mother struggling to keep the conversation going. Great Aunt Virginia remained as poised and genteel as ever, and she was the first to stand. After hugging her tightly, I lugged my suitcase out into the hall and we rode the grimy elevator down to the lobby. The street outside looked just as grubby as before, and four swarthy teenage boys lounged on Great Aunt Virginia's vandalized concrete steps. They stared at us as we passed, but a minute later we drove off, rather enthusiastically, I thought. Father seemed to be in a hurry, and Mother questioned him over and over, demanding to know how he could put me, his only twelve-year-old daughter, alone on a train ... and not even remember.

"That weird Virginia must've had something to do with it," Father growled. "I've never had any problem remembering things unless she was around."

I grinned, but I said nothing all the way home.

My room seemed uncomfortably large as I stepped

inside and closed my door. The plain white walls, glossy posters of my favorite hip-hop stars, and even my soft, comfortable bed looked very mass-produced and unattractive. I dropped my suitcase and flopped onto the bed, which didn't host a single stuffed animal; I'd put them all into a box when a snooty girl that I didn't even like made fun of them at my tenth birthday party. I grabbed my remote and clicked on the TV, found one of my favorite shows, and relaxed, trying to enjoy my return to normalcy. But I couldn't get comfortable, and the canned laughter of my favorite show seemed suddenly artificial, the constant jokes lame. Even the moments of deep emotional tension seemed forced and ludicrous, and looked antic when I momentarily flicked on the mute button. I changed the channel to my favorite music video station, which I liked to watch, but the rhythmic lyrics sounded like Great Aunt Virginia's jump rope rhymes. I frowned and dropped my remote; reality suddenly seemed dull and boring compared to live dancing marionettes and magic tea sets. I wondered what Great Aunt Virginia was doing, if she was in her apartment or in Arcadia, going off with Hiram, Muskay, Princess Gracely, and Falcon. Unhappily, I wondered what fun I was missing. I couldn't even call Great Aunt Virginia because she didn't have a phone, and I couldn't email her; that was preposterous.

I grabbed my suitcase and got out the jump rope. To my delight, right under the jump rope, I found the long green dress with the black vest and white ribbons. As I picked it up, I found two other long dresses under it, one a faded pink paisley, the other bright red and very thick: velvet, with a wide white collar and white button-down cuffs. I smiled brightly, smoothed them straight, and hung all three in my closet to keep them from wrinkling. I daren't let anyone see me wearing them, but having them nearby made me feel warm.

Being August, there was nothing to do, so I opened my laptop and logged online. I quickly scanned and deleted Mom's many frantic emails demanding to know where I was, and found two new messages from my best friend, Hilary Martin, who was already practicing to be a high school cheerleader despite that we were both in middle school. Hilary's email said that she'd heard through several notoriously-unreliable sources that a certain popular girl had gotten splashed by a water balloon at the mall by her first boyfriend three days after she broke it off with him. Two days ago news like this would've delighted me, but now it just seemed pointless.

Frustrated, I picked up the jump rope. My room wasn't tiny, but if I started jumping rope then I'd be certain to hit something, and my bouncing would knock pictures off of walls and be heard throughout our condo; our downstairs neighbor would certainly complain. But where could I practice, if not here? If I practiced anywhere else then someone might see me. What would happen if someone saw my jump rope glowing, or the gold-silver sparkles of its spherical magic shield?

I glanced up at the TV as a new video started; those singers and musicians were rich and famous. If I could do real magic, then I'd be richer and more famous than any of them. I'd be the richest and most-famous person in the world. Dreams cascaded upon me like waterfalls of cash and prizes and celebrity; everyone would want to know me. I'd be on TV every day. Books would be written about me. Movies made. I could write my own ticket, do anything that I wanted, travel the world, and experience every dream that I'd ever had. And all that I had to do was jump rope!

The biggest smile spread across my face. I lifted up my jump rope and felt its power in my hand: glory, wealth, and notoriety all combined in one simple woven cord. I knew all of the chants ...

My smile vanished: I didn't know the chants. Great Aunt Virginia knew the chants, and had only told me a few. But that wouldn't matter: once I'd shown them what I could do, they'd get the rest out of her. Even Great Aunt Virginia couldn't say no to a million dollars.

Or could she? Great Aunt Virginia had possessed these secrets since she was younger than I. She could've been infinitely wealthy long ago. She could've had servants and fame and traveled the world. She could've been the most famous person in the world. She'd chosen not to. *Why? To protect a bunch of dolls?*

It didn't matter. There were men, bad men, who could get anything out of anybody. They'd get Great Aunt Virginia to reveal her secrets.

Then I imagined Great Aunt Virginia trapped in some dark basement, surrounded by thugs, her secrets beaten from her; I couldn't allow that. And worse, I pictured myself bound to the chair beside her, the thugs beating me. How could I stop them? My shield charm was draining, exhausting; I couldn't keep it up for long. And when it failed, once they took away my jump rope, then I'd be only their helpless twelve-year-old victim.

No; I couldn't do that to Great Aunt Virginia or to myself. Revealing my magic would be the death of both of us, but there had to be a way, a safe way, to get everything that I wanted.

Patience, I told myself; I wasn't ready. Besides, once I knew all of the chants, then I wouldn't need Great Aunt Virginia anymore. But what of the dolls? What about Arcadia? If I made their existence public, then everyone would want to go there. Those same ruthless thugs that didn't care who they hurt: *could dancing marionettes survive what they'd do to them?*

I had to think this out carefully. Until I knew what I was going to do, I couldn't risk anyone finding out. Millions of kids jumped rope all over the world; if the magic chants ever got posted on the internet, then

Arcadia would be overrun by reckless kids going wild. Worse, once everyone knew about it, my only chance at being a celebrity would vanish. What would be special about me if everyone could enter Arcadia?

Then I remembered: I couldn't enter Arcadia. I needed Great Aunt Virginia's tea set. No, I wasn't ready to reveal what I knew to anyone. I needed to know more.

I opened an Instant Mail window and saw Hilary online.

Audrey> Hi

Hilary> Where u been?

Audrey> Visiting family

Hilary> Sucks

Audrey> Yea. I need to sneak off tomorrow without my parents knowing. OK if I say I'm at your house?

Hilary> Won't be home. Mom taking me shopping

Audrey> That's OK

Hilary> Where u going?

Audrey> Baltimore

Hilary> How?

Audrey> Can't say

Hilary> You crazy?

Audrey> Maybe. Must explain in person. TTYL8R

Hilary> Tell me!

I closed the window and my laptop. Hilary would be angry, but I didn't dare tell her more ... not yet. I stood up and lifted my jump rope. Maybe if I jumped really lightly ...

Holding the rope shortened, I managed to not hit the ceiling on my first swing, but its slap on my carpet was louder than I'd expected. Maybe if I recited the chant really quickly ...

I froze. *The chant!* How could I not have written it down?

"Two steps, four steps,
Six steps, eight..."

No, that was the healing chant that I'd used on Falcon. What was the chant to take me back to Great Aunt Virginia's place?

"Audrey! Audrey! Lover of dolls!"

No, that was the song that the marionettes had sung. I'd forgotten the magic chant! How could I be so stupid?

For hours I stormed about my room, furious with myself. My one chance for greatness was gone! I'd blown it! I hated myself!

All evening I wracked my brain, trying to remember the chants. They'd been so simple, so easy; I'd not thought that I could forget them. What if I just kinda remembered them? Did every word have to be exact?

In the living room, Mother and Father started shouting, and then a door slammed; Father was gone again, probably away for the night. Out getting drunk,

Mother often said, but her voice always seemed hesitant, tired, lacking conviction whenever she spoke of his absences.

Early the next morning, I told Mother that Hilary's mom was taking us shopping at the mall. No longer crying, but in an eerie, silent distractedness, Mother nodded and gave me ten dollars while she sat staring out of the window. I took the money and fled, but one block away, I walked right past Hilary's apartment and headed for our school. Most of the school was closed, but summer school was still open for the kids who didn't study enough, and no one would suspect a child behind a school carrying a jump rope.

"Audrey!"

I turned; Hilary, her dark eyes glaring, was running to catch up with me.

"Why didn't you answer me?" Hilary demanded as she ran closer. "I was IM'ing you all last night."

"Oh. Sorry, I wasn't online."

"Why not?"

I stared at Hilary; black hair and dark brown skin, staring at me with deep chocolate eyes bulging under angry brows. She was quite pretty when she wasn't glaring, her hair in tight braids, and every stitch that she wore bore a designer label, or she wouldn't let it touch her. Hilary had high ambitions and tended to be bossy, if you let her get into her stride.

"Father left again last night," I said. "He didn't come home."

"Sorry," Hilary said, and her huffiness faded a little. "You coming to the mall?"

"I can't."

"What's that? A jump rope?"

"Yea."

"What for?"

"Um ... jumping."

"Why?"

"Oh, my ... Great Aunt Virginia gave it to me."

"Is she the one who lives in Baltimore?"

"Yes."

"You're not really planning to go there ..."

"I have to."

"Walking?"

"I ... I don't know."

"What's wrong with you?"

"Nothing."

"You're acting weird."

"I have to go."

"What's going on?"

"I ... I can't say."

"Tell me!"

"I'll see you later."

I turned away and started to walk.

"Where are you going?" Hilary demanded, and when I didn't reply: "My mom will tell your mom!"

I gritted my teeth and turned back to face her.

"I'm not going anywhere!"

"What are you hiding?"

"Nothing!"

"Then come to the mall."

As usual, Hilary got her way. I reluctantly acquiesced, as I'd already told Mother that I'd be with Hilary, and Mother was likely to check up on me after yesterday's disappearance. We rode to the mall in the back seat of their luxury SUV. Michael, Hilary's younger brother, rode up front with his mom. Hilary kept casting dark looks at me while her mom spewed local minor-celebrity gossip; Hilary's stepfather was a local T.V. weatherman and her mom felt that any sentence was squandered unless she could impress her listeners by dropping at least one semi-famous name and, of course, the dropped-name was wasted unless she could attest that she knew them personally. Her social circle used to impress me until her sheer repetition of semi-important friends grew annoying.

Inside the mall, while her mother shopped for back-to-school shoes for Michael, Hilary confronted me in whispers.

"What's so important that you can't tell your best friend?"

"It's not like that."

"You're keeping secrets ... and carrying a jump rope."

I stared at Hilary. She was mad at me, but all that I could think of was Great Aunt Virginia going to Arcadia, leaving me behind.

"Something ... happened," I whispered softly. "Something ... important ... that could make me ... make us ... rich and famous."

"What ...?"

"It's ... my Great Aunt Virginia."

"Is she rich and famous?"

"She could be ... but she chooses not to ..."

"That's insane! How can ...?"

"That's what I can't tell you. It's ... something that she has ... something that she knows."

"Why can't you tell me?"

"Because ... if I keep it secret, then she'll give it to me."

Hilary's eyes popped, but remained shadowed by disbelief.

"I have to go."

"You can't leave ...!"

"I can ... if you help."

"How?"

"Let's go to the bathroom."

Hilary's mom made us stay with her until Michael's new shoes were purchased, and then she waited outside the mall bathroom while Hilary and I went in. It was still early, so the mall was mostly empty, and I quickly checked the stalls to make sure that we were alone. Then I uncoiled my jump rope.

"What are you doing?" Hilary demanded.

"Either blowing your mind or making a total fool of myself," I said. "Whatever happens, swear that you'll never tell anyone what you're about to see."

"You've lost it."

"Swear."

"Swear what?"

"Never mind; it's our path to wealth and fame ... if you can keep your mouth shut."

Hilary stared uncomprehendingly. I ignored her and tried to focus: this was my only chance. If I couldn't remember Great Aunt Virginia's chant this time then I'd fail forever. I flipped the jump rope over my head and skipped it once, twice, three times. I concentrated; I'd hoped that the slapping of the rope would jog my memory, but nothing came. Hilary stared disbelieving, appalled. I kept trying, but to no avail.

'The magic's in the play, not the tea,' Great Aunt Virginia had said.

I gave up trying to remember. I'd jump-roped all the time when I was younger; I was quite good at it and knew all the variations. I'd sang countless jump rope songs, most of which I'd made up myself. I concentrated as hard as I could and just invented the words.

"Great Aunt Virginia
I need you

To your house now
I must fly
Great Aunt Virginia
Help me now
Summon your magic
Bring me to you."

Nothing happened save that Hilary said something sarcastic, but I ignored her and focused. This was my only hope. It had to work. I repeated my rhyme again and again, and then Hilary's scream echoed terribly in the tiled mall bathroom. I looked up to see her and the toilet stalls fading slightly with each pass of my gold-and-silver sparkling jump rope ... and then they were gone.

Chapter 5

Gathering Information

Shadows darkened as the glare of the bathroom's neon lights vanished. Two plain, high, red-brick walls appeared lining a narrow passage littered with filthy old boxes, moldy furniture, and a large green metal dumpster. After a frightened moment of disorientation, I recognized the alley outside of my bedroom window at Great Aunt Virginia's house. I stopped jump-roping and ran out of the alley, and then up the concrete steps, past six boys who eyed me threateningly.

"Hey, girl, what's your hurry?" one boy asked, an unpleasant sneer in his voice.

"Yea, hang with us," another boy grinned nastily.

I grabbed the doorknob and twisted it, but the door was locked. The boys laughed and again invited me to join them. Desperately I scanned the row of white buttons, pressed the one marked 'V. Darby', and waited anxiously. If Great Aunt Virginia was in Arcadia, what would I do?

No reply came. I pressed her button again and held it.

"Nobody home," one boy said with a sinister laugh.

"Party time!" a large, muscular boy stood up, and soon all of the boys were standing, leaning close to me, leering and chuckling nastily.

I filled my lungs and screamed as loudly as I could, not panicked, but purposefully. These boys were older and bigger than I, but their smiles faded as every passerby on the sidewalk instantly snapped their head to look at us, and more heads stuck out of windows, seeking the source of the disturbance.

The boys' smiles faded; their fun depended on my timidity, but I was a city girl. I screamed again, and they forced a discomforted laugh, and then walked down the steps with a dozen adults watching them intently. One old man with gray hair in a brown sweater stopped and glared directly at them from the sidewalk, and the defeated boys averted their eyes as they slunk past him, struggling to keep up their image of toughness. The old man kept staring until the boys vanished inside the next building, and then he turned to look at me. I nodded my thanks to him and he nodded back, and then he continued on his way.

"Audrey, what's the meaning of this?" a familiar voice spoke as the door opened behind me.

I hugged Great Aunt Virginia tightly, terribly relieved.

"Sorry," I said.

Minutes later, safe in her apartment, surrounded by tiny figurines and polished wooden antiques, I started to relax.

"I was afraid that you'd left without me," I said.

"I thought you'd come properly dressed," Great Aunt Virginia said.

"I wanted to, but I can't wear those dresses in public."

"Why not?"

How could I explain modern fashions to someone wearing Victorian stays in her dress? I shrugged, slumping my shoulders.

"Posture, child: a lady maintains good posture."

I straightened my shoulders and then glanced expectantly at the tea set.

"Are we going back to Arcadia?"

"As soon as you make the tea."

"I thought that we didn't need tea ..."

"Good tea makes every journey easier, and it helps us stay longer; we have much to do today."

Great Aunt Virginia took me into the kitchen and set her teapot on the stove, then offered to let me choose my own recipe. I scoured through her tan ceramic jars while she quoted the effects of each from memory.

"Dried tarragon seeds stimulate the appetite.

Mulberry twigs promote circulation and banish tiredness. Mint is sweet and good for the stomach. Dogbane relieves fever, gallstones, and dropsy. Thyme leaves ease sore throats and soothes coughs. Valerian root relieves anxiety and insomnia, is useful in hysteria, cures sores and pimples, and is still a widely-used sedative in Europe. Bistort root is a strong astringent: when directly applied to a wound, its dried powder stops bleeding. Rosemary leaves and twigs are good for circulation and stimulate weak nerves, useful for headache and depression. Parsley root, leaves, and seeds are a rich source of vitamin C and good for dieting. Mistletoe is for love, but it's dangerous; Mistletoe is poisonous unless properly administered: leave it be."

Finally I chose a mixture, including more mint and parsley leaves than Great Aunt Virginia recommended, but she allowed me to put them into the mortar, with a pinch of cinnamon, and grind them with the pestle. As I ground, I used the opportunity to ask the question most-burning in my mind.

"I forgot the chant to bring me here. I made one up ... and it worked. The first time that we went to Arcadia, you had me mix the tea and breathe on it, and then we came without any."

"At your age, would you have believed that my tea was magic if it hadn't had a mysterious origin? Would you have believed enough to heal Falcon if you hadn't thought that my rhyme was a magical chant?"

"Then ... the magic is in believing?"

"Magic comes from many sources," Great Aunt Virginia said. "Some kids find Arcadia through simple play, and others find it through desperation to get away from unbearable situations. Some find Arcadia through faith. Magic is all around us, everywhere that the pure-at-heart look for it, but for people whose hearts have darkened, for those who've turned from joy to bitterness, the only doorway from this world ... is the exit of mortality, and that door is one-way."

We spooned the powdered tea into the pot, stirred the water, and Great Aunt Virginia smiled.

"Just enough time for you to dress while it steeps."

Ten minutes later, I was sitting in a long, soft black skirt, with a bright blue ruffled top with spaghetti-straps over my shoulders, holding my jump rope and sitting on the hard red-cushioned couch while Great Aunt Virginia poured tea.

"Doesn't Audrey look especially nice today?" Great Aunt Virginia asked the three dolls set around her tiny table.

"Princess Gracely, did you change your hairstyle?" I asked. "It looks very pretty."

Great Aunt Virginia smiled. She sat beside me on the couch and we lifted our tea cups together. I watched the dolls as I drank, anticipating the heady dizziness as it stole over me. Disoriented, I could've sworn that Muskay turned his ceramic head slightly, and Hiram's furry bear-arm lifted his blue and pink patterned teacup off the table, and then they were gone.

Stomp! Stomp! Stomp!

The strange noise came from a line of fifteen small, brightly-painted tin soldiers who marched into our tiny, cramped room in perfect unison, slamming their feet on the polished wooden floor. No table stood here, no grown-up sized version of the pink and blue teacups; I was standing, not sitting, bent over in a tiny room whose miniature doors surrounded a wood-railed balcony whose height was even with my elbow. I was in a miniature version of a great hall in a southern mansion, like a giant doll house, which must've seemed huge to its eight-inch tall tin soldiers, but whose ceiling pressed hard against the top of my head. Great Aunt Virginia was stooping badly beside me, her lips tightly pursed, and Princess Gracely and Muskay were sitting cross-legged on the floor. Princess Gracely's wide, flowing white dress covered most of the floor and half of Muskay, who was grinning slyly in his tight red and black checked outfit.

On the balcony, beside each door, stood a polished tin soldier at attention, and side-by-side stood seven garishly-uniformed nutcracker dolls, each much taller than the tin soldiers, with comically bushy beards, mustaches, and eyebrows of fake fur. All were staring at us.

"Owners?" The center-most nutcracker cried in

disbelief, his wide wooden mouth flapping as if on a hinge. "Unauthorized admittance to council chambers? Disgraceful! Irregular!"

"Please, forgive them, General Walnut," Princess Gracely said. "They were drawn to us."

"Against regulations," General Walnut said, and all the other nutcrackers bobbed their heads in agreement. "Improper protocol."

"We're sorry, but they've come to help," Princess Gracely continued.

"Help?" General Walnut asked. "Civilians plan a military mission? Tish-tosh! Initiate a formal investigation? Impossible: this is a military activity."

"Well, you don't seem to be doing much, do you?" Muskay asked.

"General Walnut, you remember me, don't you?" Great Aunt Virginia asked.

"Of course!" General Walnut rolled his eyes. "Presumptuous that we could forget your past commendations. Inappropriate."

"Could we have a report?" Great Aunt Virginia asked. "Just a report to ... calm the civilians?"

"Finally: a proper request. Very well. Report this: everything is fine."

"Even the three missing squads?" Muskay asked.

"Failure to report in is not missing," General Walnut insisted.

"What about the babies?" Princess Gracely

asked.

"Babies? What babies?"

"Exactly," Muskay sneered.

"The babies that have been missing for a year," Princess Gracely said.

"Yes, we know all about that."

"Well?" Muskay asked.

"Well ... what?"

"What are you doing about the missing babies?"

"Doing?" General Walnut asked. "Who said that we were doing anything?"

"Surely you're looking for them!" Princess Gracely insisted.

"Not a military matter," General Walnut said. "We investigated it thoroughly; found no evidence of foul play."

"No foul play?" Muskay asked. "What? A hundred baby dolls just decided to up and leave their homes ... and their caregivers?"

"No evidence to the contrary," General Walnut said.

"But where are they?" Princess Gracely asked.

"How should I know?" General Walnut asked. "Babies, civilians, are free to go anywhere they like."

"General Walnut, surely you searched for them?" Great Aunt Virginia asked.

"Of course!" General Walnut said. "Every squad on patrol has been ordered to report any baby sightings for nearly a year. We've a whole division on stand-by, waiting for a sighting."

"A whole division ... standing around waiting ... for a year?" Muskay asked. "You didn't send them out to help search?"

"Waste of resources," General Walnut said. "We can't order troops into the field without clear evidence of provocation; the populace would panic."

"The populace is panicking!" Muskay shouted.

"Excuse me," I said timidly.

General Walnut and all the other nutcracker dolls turned to look at me, surprise on their painted faces.

"Who is this?" General Walnut demanded. "Unauthorized personnel on a military compound ...?"

"General Walnut, this is Audrey, my great niece," Great Aunt Virginia said.

"We've no file on any Great Niece Audrey. She can't just come in here ..."

"The jump rope is hers." Muskay said.

"What? A transfer? A promotion? Why wasn't a report filed? Dereliction! Insubordination!"

"General," I asked, interrupting. "The squads that ... failed to report ... were they searching for the baby dolls?"

"Aha!" Muskay cried.

General Walnut stiffly paled, then turned

around. The other nutcracker dolls huddled close around him and whispered fervently, their bejeweled and tall-feathered wooden hats knocking loudly against each other, hiding their whispers behind an infernal clacking of knocking and hinged jaws. Over a minute they hissed and squabbled, in which it seemed like every one of them was talking and not one was listening, and then, just as suddenly, they broke apart and resumed their previous positions.

"Ummm ...," General Walnut began, "... it has recently come to our attention ... before this meeting, I assure you ... that since every squad has standing orders to report all sightings of any babies ... and regular patrols are constantly sent to search for enemies, in accordance with General Order 241.475, as clearly ..."

"General!" Great Aunt Virginia, Princess Gracely, and Muskay shouted.

General Walnut cleared his throat, and then slowly looked up at us.

"All three squads who failed to report ... were searching for the babies."

"Do you have any idea what might've caused the disappearances?" Muskay asked.

"None at all," General Walnut admitted. "Official scouts have reported nothing. Quite mysterious, actually."

"Let's get out of here," Muskay said, heaving a disgusted sigh.

"General Walnut, thank you for this audience,"

Princess Gracely said.

"Anytime, anytime!" General Walnut nodded politely.

Muskay reached up and knocked on the ceiling three times. Suddenly something loudly scraped, and one whole wall opened up. Hiram stood outside, holding open the wall like a great hinged door. Muskay jumped out and then reached in to assist Princess Gracely, who slid out with amazing dexterity. I followed, and Great Aunt Virginia crawled out behind me, almost bent in half. As we stepped out, Hiram closed the wall, resealing the official nutcracker's military hall.

I stared amazed. A thin, two-foot-high crenellated stone wall enclosed a vast courtyard complete with long rows of tiny barracks and other buildings. The palisade surrounded at least a square quarter-mile and was filled with hundreds, perhaps a thousand tin soldiers, all marching about in groups, standing posted at gates or in signal towers. In the distance stood a huge corral filled with tiny rocking and hobby horses.

"What a waste of time!" Muskey scoffed.

"Not at all," Princess Gracely said. "We learned that all the missing squads were searching for the baby dolls."

"Falcon was right," Hiram said.

"Where's Falcon?" I asked, looking around.

"Oh, he won't come near the fort," Hiram said.

"He says that he won't do any work, so why should he watch others doing it?"

"Let's find him," Princess Gracely said. "Then we can begin."

On the far side of a nearby hill, we found Falcon resting in the shade of a small tree. Falcon was dressed differently today, now wearing a blood-red tuxedo, but with the same tired face and beak-like nose.

"I knew it," Falcon scowled after Muskay described their meeting. "Those regulatory morons ...!"

"We know enough to keep investigating," Princess Gracely said.

"What's left to investigate?" Hiram asked. "Knowing that the squads were searching for the baby dolls doesn't help us."

"Perhaps it does," Great Aunt Virginia said. "Audrey, what does it mean if the three squads that vanished were looking for the baby dolls?"

"Me?" I asked.

"Unless you'd rather go home."

"No, no," I said, and I thought about it, and then my eyes widened in realization. "It means that ... because all of the squads were looking for baby dolls ... the fact that those three squads were the ones to vanish ... means that they were the ones closest to finding the missing dolls!"

"Exactly," Great Aunt Virginia said.

"Brilliant!" Hiram exclaimed.

"So, all we need to do is to go back to the site where

the last attack happened and look for clues," Muskay said.

Everyone nodded, smiling, and we all turned to face Falcon. Falcon's smile faltered as he noticed our stares.

"N-now, w-wait a minute," Falcon stammered. "I'm not going back ...! I almost got killed ...!"

"We need you to lead us," Princess Gracely said.

"I can tell you ...," Falcon said.

"The exact spot?" Muskay asked. "I thought that you said that it was dark ..."

"It was, I mean ...," Falcon argued. "You don't need me ...!"

"Fine," Great Aunt Virginia snapped haughtily. "We'll go without Falcon. I'm not sure if we'll find the right place, which means that we may never rescue the baby dolls, but that's not Falcon's fault. We'll just leave him right here, all alone, the only surviving witness to the last attack of ... whatever it was. We have the jump rope, which means he'll be apart from his only protection, but I'm sure that whatever attacked him isn't sneaking around, watching, just waiting for the chance to pick off their only witness ..."

Great Aunt Virginia stalked off down the hill. One by one, with baleful glares at Falcon, we followed. Unsurprisingly, before we reached the bottom of the hill, Falcon trailed after us, grumbling under his breath.

"Bravery is for idiots," Falcon complained.

At the bottom of the hill, Great Aunt Virginia led us into a thick forest which had a narrow trail winding through it. This forest was dense, but bright beams of sunlight streamed through its canopy, and rich scents and many bright blossoms delighted our senses. As we followed the wide trail, small shapes rustled the underbrush; rabbits, cats, and dogs dashed all about in the shrubs, but they weren't real; all were stuffed animals like the ones on my bed at Great Aunt Virginia's house and the ones stored in the box in my closet. Seeing them running about the woods, colored fake fur and bright button eyes, I smiled, and suddenly a large, real-life unicorn trotted into view, eyed us, and bowed its gold-ribboned horn. I stared at it as we walked past; this unicorn must have a loving owner in our world. Then an owl hooted loudly, not a stuffed animal but a real live owl, and it winged off between the tall trunks until it was gone.

Guilt swelled as I thought of my stuffed animals that I'd put away after my tenth birthday. They were my dolls; I'd played with them since before I could remember. Had they been real animals until I'd stopped loving them?

We wandered for an hour down the wooded trail before the trees ended. The forest opened up upon a wide, amazing hill.

"Isn't it beautiful?" Princess Gracely sighed.

I stared agape in total disbelief.

Chapter 6

Audrey Takes Charge

The bright afternoon sun shone down upon a wide, grassy hill brightly colored by beautiful flowers. The great hill had two magnificent marble doors built into the very side of it, but the doors were only three feet tall with a miniature stone stairs leading up to them. Many wide, white-framed windows with matching shutters dotted the hillside near the doors, all of which were open. The hill also had, in seemingly random order, countless tiny, dark, round, overgrown windows beside small openings that looked like caves tunneled right into the side of the hill. But the most startling aspect of the hill was that hundreds of tall tufts of shockingly-colored hair were moving about among the vibrant flowers; tiny, hairy dolls were scrambling about the hill, playing ball, rolling in the grass, or just running hand-in-hand, joyously laughing. These dolls were very strange; short and stubby, only five inches tall, with wide ears and toothy grins, bright, energetic eyes, and thick, neon-colored tufts of hair which rose over their heads as if combed straight up, doubling their height or more. Not one doll was wearing a stitch of clothes.

"What are they?" I asked.

"Trolls," Hiram said.

"Stupid ...," Muskay began.

"They're precious and innocent," Princess Gracely waved Muskay silent.

"You're too young to remember," Great Aunt Virginia said to me. "Troll dolls were popular when I was a little girl. Everyone thought that trolls were lucky. Their fad didn't last long, but even beloved trolls always remained dolls in Arcadia. Trolls are always happy and playful."

Loud applause burst from the bank of a nearby pond amid delighted whoops and cheers. A small crowd of trolls ran up from the stream, laughing, following a group of seven trolls whose hair and bodies were soaking wet and who were running up the hill carrying a large, wriggling trout over their heads.

"Oh, yes; trolls are very strong," Great Aunt Virginia added. "Nearly indestructible, so almost every troll ever made is still here."

"Should we ask them about the missing babies?" Hiram asked, scratching his thick beard.

"Ask all you want," Muskay said. "I'll be amazed if one troll understands the question."

The fish-bearers and their jubilant crowd ran up the hill and vanished into the big marble doors before we reached the nearest trolls, a boy and girl troll, although only their exuberant faces belied any real difference. She had glittering green eye-shadow over her exaggerated eyelids and thick, ruby-red lips, while his boyish face mirrored her vacant, happy expression, and both their cheeks shined rosy-pink. The boy troll had brilliant bluebird-colored hair, the girl troll solar-bright yellow, both combed straight up in an explosion of shiny mane. They were tossing back and forth a perfectly round white rock like a ball, but they stopped as we approached.

"Hello, my friends," Princess Gracely performed a perfect curtsey.

"Hi!" both trolls said with exuberant smiles, and both tried to mimic Princess Gracely's curtsey though neither came close; the boy troll almost fell over.

"We're investigating the disappearances of the baby dolls," Princess Gracely continued. "And three squads of tin soldiers are also missing. Have you seen anything strange lately?"

Beaming smiles, both trolls stood looking at her, quite unperturbed by her question.

"You're pretty," the girl troll said.

The boy troll nodded vigorously.

"Thank you," Princess Gracely said. "Is there

someone of authority that I can talk to?"

Neither troll responded, but their smiles continued.

"Who rules the trolls?" Hiram asked.

"Who is your chief?" Muskay asked.

The trolls exchanged glances, but both continued to smile silently.

"They're like children," I said.

"Then you should treat them like children," Great Aunt Virginia advised.

I stared at their beaming faces.

"Who punishes trolls when they misbehave?" I asked.

Both smiles vanished instantly, replaced by shy, fearful glances.

"We've been good!" the boy troll insisted in a high, worried tone.

"Who punishes bad trolls?" I asked more forcefully.

Both trolls pointed up to the main marble doors opening from the side of the hill.

"Thank you," I said. "You're both very good."

Wan smiles lightened their nervous expressions, and as one they seemed to realize that their part was done. Hand-in-hand, they ran off toward the small lake, taking their white rock with them. We turned toward the marble doors and walked straight up the hill. Inside one of the many hand-dug doors that we passed, I spied crude furniture woven from sticks like a bird's nest, but carefully shaped into couches, chairs, and tables, filling the inside of a rough-hewn chamber. Yet, as we reached the main marble doorway, which had many tiny steps leading to it, each barely wide enough to rest my fingertips on, we found two relatively massive doors, each three feet tall and a foot wide, which opened upon a masterfully-built hall lit by tiny torches. Inside the hall, many trolls were gathered, and in its center was a round firepit of glowing coals, atop which the freshly-caught fish was already laid. Some trolls were busily scooping up flaming embers with long spoons and shoveling them on top of the cooking fish.

"People of Troll Hill!" Princess Gracely called. "Please, we beg an audience."

This request was met with delighted surprise. Many trolls hurried out, all with eager faces.

"Who is your leader?" Princess Gracely asked.

All of the trolls turned and pointed to a thick-set older troll with pure white hair.

"Me cook," he said.

"A pleasure to meet you, Master Cook," Princess Gracely curtseyed again. "I am named Gracely, and my friends are Virginia, Audrey, Hiram, Muskay, and Falcon. What are you called?"

"Cook," he replied, and many of the trolls bobbed their heads in agreement.

"Well met, good ... Master Cook. We've heard many reports of bad things. Have you, or any of your people, seen any bad things?"

Cook and the other trolls looked at each other,

some looking worried, others just confused. Then one troll spoke up.

"I'm Stoney," he spoke slowly, his voice deeper than any of the other trolls. "What kind of bad things?"

Stoney was slightly taller and much heavier, with a round stomach bulging twice as much as the other trolls. His tall hair was even thicker than the others, far less kempt, and shocking pink. Upon his right cheek was an ugly, jagged scar.

"Any kind of bad things, Mr. Stoney," Princess Gracely answered. "The baby dolls are still missing ... and three squads of tin soldiers have vanished."

"That's bad," Stoney said slowly. "Can you keep bad away from Troll Hill?"

"We don't yet know who's causing the trouble."

"That's also bad," Stoney said. "Bad people like trolls; we are gladly helpful, but slow to question."

"You're good people," Great Aunt Virginia said.

"Goodness can cause suffering," Stoney said, looking at her. "My scar reminds me of the bad times: Changers, Hag, and Punch."

"You're very wise ... for a troll," Great Aunt Virginia said. "Those times were long ago; we're trying to keep them from returning."

"Make bad go away," Stoney said.

"We will try," Princess Gracely promised.

Stoney nodded once, his huge pink hair flopping forward, then back, and then he turned and walked back into the hall through the great doors. The other trolls looked confused, but slowly followed him inside.

"Well, that didn't help," Muskay said.

"I didn't expect that it would, but as we were passing by ...," Princess Gracely said.

"It was the right thing to do," Hiram said. "At least we warned them ..."

"Warned?" Muskay sneered. "Stupid trolls! They'd help the devil himself if he asked politely."

"That's true, I'm afraid," Great Aunt Virginia said. "Evil has a fondness for deceiving the innocent, and trolls are never suspicious."

"Let's keep walking," Princess Gracely suggested. "We still have a long way to go."

We resumed our trek over and down the back of Troll Hill, watched intently by many curious trolls, some peeking out from their many crudely-dug holes. A few tried to follow us, but Muskay and Falcon chased them back before they wandered too far from their homes and got lost. As we marched across a wide field, which was unusually smooth and well-tended, I sidled up beside Great Aunt Virginia.

"What are Changers, Hag, and Punch?" I asked.

"Old threats that we struggled against long ago," Great Aunt Virginia said. "It doesn't happen often, but most dolls are very weak; it doesn't take much of a challenge to threaten them, and some invaders have caused widespread destruction. Changers, Hag, and Punch were the worst, so bad that even some trolls can't forget them."

"But what are they?"

"Changers are change-bots, toy robots that transform from one shape to another. Like most action figures, they're very violent, composed of two warring sides eternally battling, and their passage through Arcadia ruined several cities and killed many dolls. Eventually we forced them out, but the hand-puppets were repairing their damage for years. Hag was an exceedingly strange creature, a mysterious, powerful voodoo doll. She enchanted many dolls and made them do unspeakable things. We never knew where she came from, or where she vanished to after we burned her boat, but we never saw her again. Punch was a very old doll, huge and commanding, the most popular doll in medieval Europe. Without his wife, Judy, Punch tried to overthrow Arcadia and banish all of the new dolls; Punch was jealous of the popularity that he'd lost, but Judy helped us overthrow him in the end, and we banished him from the world of dolls. It was very sad: Judy cried and cried."

"Where did he go?"

"Back to our world," Great Aunt Virginia said. "Punch was my first challenge when Great Aunt Annie brought me to Arcadia."

"What else have you fought?"

"Too many to remember," Great Aunt Virginia sighed wearily. "Corrosion beasts, monster dolls, and something that called itself a wrestler whose arms stretched ridiculously far. But such times are few and fleeting; usually my visits to Arcadia are pleasant and peaceful."

We walked several miles across beautiful meadows, crossing many small, swift-flowing streams that we could drink from, and finally came to a dark forest, sparse and rugged. Many of its trees looked dead.

"This is it," Falcon said, frowning.

I glanced warily about, but the only threat seemed to be the countless sharp thorns whose long branches loomed out from the menacing forest's shadows as if trying to grab us. I was glad that I was wearing sneakers, although running in this long skirt would seem restrictive; anything could be hiding in the dark recesses of these woods; the black-barked trees were huge and their nearly leafless lower branches intertwined, as if grappling in tree-fashion. The aged bark of their fat trunks was strangely knotted, and nothing fruitful hung from their spiky branches, nor did the piled, rotting thickets of fallen branches and dead leaves contain any evidence of wholesome reproduction. Weeds alone thrived amid the trees' thick, knotty roots, which vanished under the soil and then rose back up to trip unwary travelers. I coughed: the air beneath these branches was arid and stifling, hard to breathe, fumigated with rottenness. No birdsong filled the air, nor were any live or stuffed animals flitting around its wretched undergrowth. The whole forest seemed poisoned with malice.

"What is this place?" I asked.

"The Aging Forest," Hiram said.

"No one comes here," Muskay said.

"These trees welcome no one," Princess Gracely said. "A great battle happened here once, long ago, in times so ancient that only the trees remember. The lonely wanderers tell of a vast clear-cutting, a fire, and an eternal hatred that blackens tree-hearts to their cores."

"Let's finish this," Great Aunt Virginia said. "Falcon, where were you attacked?"

"Over here, I think," Falcon said.

Falcon led us down a long trail until we heard the rushing sounds of a great river. I spied great white frothing rapids behind a row of thick black trunks; a wild river, narrow, rushing very fast, splashing high over jagged rocks that rose in the center of its path, churning the river into a violent, white-water deathtrap.

"You fell into that?" I asked Facon.

"Not on purpose, but it saved my life," he said. "Look; there's my footprints."

We all stopped before a soft patch of muddy dirt. Falcon pressed one shoe into the damp soil beside one of the many footprints, and his mark matched the footprints exactly.

"So, you really did come here ...," Muskay teased.

"Enough of that," Great Aunt Virginia said. "What concerns me is that there are no monster's tracks."

Not far ahead we found more of Falcon's tracks, closely spaced together, in bare patches moistened by the river's mist. Then his footprints appeared widely spaced out.

"You were running here," Hiram said. "That's odd."

"I told you that I ran after the darkness closed in," Falcon reminded.

"Yes, but what were you running from?" Hiram asked. "There're no tracks atop yours."

We followed Falcon's tracks into the deep shadows of the trees where they grew thick about the river and there was barely enough room to squeeze between their trunks. Menacing limbs hovered over our heads, seeming to lower slightly as we stepped under them. A strong, foul reek rose from their roots.

"What a stench!" Muskay exclaimed.

"That's blood-stink," Hiram said. "Falcon's rotting blood."

"But what's this?" I asked.

The others all stared as I bent and pawed at the loose, moist dirt which showed, not footprints, but handprints and the ruts of Falcon's knees as he'd crawled toward the river. Something was strange about this dirt; it seemed to be flecked with tiny, shiny points, hard to see in the shadows of the branches. I knelt down and examined them closely.

"What is it?" Great Aunt Virginia asked.

I touched the dull points of reflection and some stuck to my hand, not threateningly. I stared amazed at the tiny reflecting sparkles.

"It's ... glitter," I said.

"Glitter?" they all asked.

I stood up, flipped out my jump rope, and took a handle in each hand. The others quickly stepped back as I began jumping, and I made up the song as I went.

"Bright light,
Shine bright!
Bring the day!
Ban the night!"

I repeated my simple chant as I jump-roped faster, concentrating as Great Aunt Virginia had taught me, and my smile brightened as the glow started, then grew stronger. I increased my speed, Single Bouncing, taking only one step between each flip of my jump rope. A great brightness erupted from its cord. Shining, my light illuminated the dark trees, the muddy ground, and purged the shadows from beneath the thick, high branches. Hiram, Falcon, Muskay, Princess Gracely, and Great Aunt Virginia gasped: tiny colored specs, mostly gold and silver, littered the whole area, brightly reflecting my jump rope's light with brilliant sparkles.

My tiredness swelled, so I quit jumping, and my magic light failed almost instantly. Princess Gracely stooped and grazed the wet weeds with her delicate fingers, and then lifted her hand, examining the glittering sparkles.

"Glitter?" Princess Gracely asked. "Not ... magic?"

"There was no glitter on me," Falcon said.

"The river probably gave you a much-needed bath," Muskay said.

"Not now, Muskay," Hiram said.

"What kind of monster trails glitter?" Princess Gracely asked.

"Something new, something that we've never seen," Great Aunt Virginia said.

"Maybe it's not glitter, but shavings of real gold and silver," Muskay suggested.

"No, this is glitter," I said. "I've played with lots of it."

"Where would a clawed monster get glitter?" Hiram asked.

"What kind of clawed monster kills people and drops glitter?" Falcon asked. "I mean, what good is glitter?"

I tried to think, but my thoughts were hazy, my sight growing blurry. Great Aunt Virginia lifted her hand to her forehead and looked suddenly pained.

"We need to go back," Great Aunt Virginia said. "Audrey is still unused to the strains of jumping. You should get back to safety as well. We found a clue; we can ponder it later."

"Safe journey to us all," Princess Gracely said.

I opened my eyes; across an antique child's

pink-and-blue tea set sat the three dolls that I loved most, Great Aunt Virginia's counterparts for Hiram, Muskay, and Princess Gracely. I smiled at them.

"Audrey, I'm very proud of you," Great Aunt Virginia said, but her voice seemed weary. "Forgive me, but I ... need some rest. Can ... can you get back home ... by yourself?"

"I think so," I assured her.

Slowly Great Aunt Virginia rose, and I realized how heavily old age was wearing upon her. She seemed very sad and stood with strained care, as if afraid that she might fall. She left her tea cup on the table and used her ebony cane to walk back into the hall, and I stayed until I heard her bedroom door close.

I glanced at the tea set, then decided that I had to get back. But I couldn't jump rope in here; one slip and I might kill some poor doll's counterpart. I changed my clothes, coiled my jump rope, went out into the hallway and, after checking to make sure that Great Aunt Virginia's front door had locked behind me, I raced down the empty stairs, rushed into the alley beside her building, and jump-roped my way back.

"Take me back, take me back!
Magic rope, don't go slack!
Take me back where I belong!
Don't make me sing another song!"

I kept repeating my rhyme as I skipped, almost fervently, concentrating as hard as I could. It seemed to take forever, but finally my rope, flashing rhythmically before my eyes, began to sparkle, and I focused even more, chanting as hard as I could. The world around me began to shift in spurts, with each pass of my jump rope, but not into my apartment. Florescent lights glared on tile; my jump rope caught on the toe of my sneakers; I stumbled, tripped, and almost fell. The white room that I was in was filled with rows of sinks and stalls: the mall bathroom, exactly where I'd left Hilary.

I took a deep breath and forced myself to relax; I was at the mall, close to home, not in Baltimore. My spell had worked; I just hadn't been specific enough. I thought about trying again, but sounds came from a stall; someone else was in here, and as I stood wondering, a woman with bulging shopping bags entered pulling a crying three year old girl. I quickly slipped past her and out.

The mall was very full, a few customers waiting just outside of the bathrooms, some talking on cell phones, others walking hurriedly past, as if in a race, or strolling leisurely, staring into each store as if seeking treasures, becoming frustrating obstacles to those in a hurry. I wondered if Hilary and her mother were still here and feared what Mother would say when I called her to pick me up.

A pair of police officers came striding through the mall in deep conversation, and then a voice shouted.

"There! With the jump rope!"

Both police officers startled, looked at me, and then broke through the crowd just as a hand grabbed my shoulder. I jerked away and then looked up to see a uniformed security guard with a puzzled expression staring at me. I wanted to shout at him for touching me, but both policemen instantly confronted me.

"Are you Audrey?" one asked.

"Yes."

His expression grew cross, and he lifted a microphone from his belt to his mouth.

"Brathers here; the missing mall-child is located."

All three of the men, and a large crowd of shoppers, stared at me until I felt decidedly uncomfortable.

"Are you injured?" Officer Brathers asked.

"No."

"Were you abducted?"

"No."

"Where have you been?"

I had no answer to this. I stood silent, very afraid. I'd been gone for hours; Hilary's mother must've been frantic. Mother would be furious.

"Her mother's in the office," the security guard said.

"Lead the way."

Following the security guard, with both officers half-a-step behind, I marched like a condemned prisoner with my eyes downcast, feeling the wondering stares of every patron in the mall. We entered an unmarked door and walked down a long, narrow, footstep-echoing hallway, up some stairs, and into an office waiting room.

Mother, Hilary, and her mother and brother were all there, with two men in suits. Both women were crying. As I entered, both jumped up and ran to embrace me, alternately blubbering and chastising me in a torn confusion of anger and tears. I tried to reassure them that I was fine, but not a word could be discerned amid their chaotic, embarrassing wails. I spied Hilary standing beside her little brother with a hateful glare that I couldn't believe any child could produce; I'd vanished and left her to explain the impossible. She'd told, I realized as I picked out the word 'Baltimore' amid the older women's babbling. I couldn't blame her, but neither could I explain where I'd gone or how I got back.

Suddenly they released me and stood back, looking behind me. I turned to see Officer Brathers staring down at me with his jaw set.

"Audrey, this is twice that you've vanished without any notice in two days," Officer Brathers said. "Where you went is not my concern. Where you're going, if it happens again, is to jail. Then you can explain these disappearances to a judge. You'll be arrested, charged, brought to trial, and convicted. You won't be the first child that I've sent to Juvenile Hall. Do you understand the consequences of your behavior?"

"Yes, sir," I said timidly.

"Good," Officer Brathers said. "We searched this mall from top to bottom, the parking lot, and the surrounding buildings. We watched you enter the mall on video tape. We've had bus drivers between here and Baltimore watching out for you. Television and radio broadcasts have been reporting Amber Alerts for hours. Where were you?"

Everyone fell silent, staring expectantly. I fought to find an answer, to say something, anything ... but nothing would excuse a twelve year old girl from vanishing in a crowded mall. I stared back dumbly, finding no words. Officer Brathers glared down at me, and then he reached back, and pulled from his belt a pair of steel handcuffs.

"No!" Mother cried. "You can't!"

Officer Brathers reconsidered, then put them away.

"I can. If she vanishes again, I'll arrest you both; failure to supervise a minor is child endangerment, a serious misdemeanor which judges have little patience for. Is that understood?"

"I waited right outside that bathroom ... there are no other exits ...!" Hilary's mother protested.

"I understand," Mother answered Officer Brathers, and he handed her a card.

"When you find out where she's been, please give me a call; I need to include it in my report."

"Yes, sir. Thank you."

Mother seized my arm in a grip that clamped off my circulation. Hilary's mother grabbed Hilary and Michael, who was still carrying the box of shoes that she'd bought him, and we left, walking as fast as Mother could go. Out into the crowded mall, and then straight to the parking lot we walked, where Mother spoke to Hilary's mother.

"Madge, I'm sorry."

"Me, too; I'm just glad she's alright."

"Talk to you later."

"Sure."

Mother dragged me off with unrivaled fury. She had every right to be angry; I kept my head bowed and tried to avoid her glare. Mother said nothing all the way home.

I was banished to my room, but their shouts penetrated my walls; Father had come home not even knowing that I was missing, found the place empty, and started to pack. Mother was screaming at him, and their yells permeated into adjacent condos. Tears burst from my eyes; my world was crumbling.

I looked up from my damp, tear-wet pillow, and glanced at my jump rope. I didn't have to let this happen: *I had magic!*

I jumped off my bed and snatched up my jump rope. I gripped the worn handles and looped the green ends around my hands to shorten it; skipping rope was harder if you didn't let it touch the floor, but I had to do it. With all of the shouting and crashing, my jumping might go unnoticed. I feared that I wasn't strong enough, and that Great Aunt Virginia wouldn't approve, but if I let Father walk out again ...

I started to jump and skipped five times before I managed to make up a chant, just letting it come.

"Make them love again,
Make them love.
Remember the good times,
Make them love."

I repeated my chant and kept jumping, trying to land easily so that I didn't shake the building. Doubts stabbed; could I chant hard enough? But I kept going, concentrating, pushing harder with all of my will. My chant grew strong, my voice demanding. I refused to give up. Sparkles started on my jump rope. My room brightened, illuminated gold and silver with the sheen tracing off my green flipping cord. I refused to stop and forced my chant; I wasn't just saving some helpless doll: my parents were real, and I couldn't bear them fighting.

"Make them love again,
Make them love.
Remember the good times,
Make them love."

My room glowed; I skipped faster, but the strain was starting to wear. I ignored it, jumped and chanted, but my muscles felt weakened and my breathing grew shallow. My head felt dizzy, disoriented, as if I'd been awake for days and couldn't keep my eyes open a moment longer. Yet I didn't stop: I kept chanting and jumping as the brilliance of my sparkles blinded my eyes. A gold and silver globe encased me. I felt suffocated, pressed in on all sides, squeezed, and it grew exponentially worse, but I was determined to never stop, the brightness of my jump rope fighting against the darkness consuming me.

The jump rope caught my toes and its next pass slapped against my ankles. I stumbled face-first, crashed to the floor, and collapsed from exhaustion. Blood burst from my nose as it smashed against my carpet, and I didn't have enough strength to lift my head. I lay gasping and panting, slowly writhing, my head pounding; never had I felt this awful.

Then I noticed the silence. No shouts were coming through the walls. *Had Father left?* Despite everything, I had to know. Ignoring my aches and will-sapping weariness, I crawled across the carpet to my door. *Had it worked …?*

Quietly I opened my door a crack. Mother and Father were hugging tight, and kissing hard, deeply and fervently. I stared for a moment, and then I fell against the inside of my door and passed out.

Chapter 7

Bitter Regrets

I awoke hungry; the scent of frying bacon filled my nostrils. Barely I recalled dragging myself to my bed sometime in the night, shivering with cold, and sliding beneath my warm blankets. Then I remembered my parents hugging and kissing, and my eyes opened wide.

I ran out into the living room and smiled to see Father sitting at our table and Mother cooking breakfast; *the old times had come back again.*

Then I saw their faces; Father's eyes were closed, his jaw set, his head bent low over his empty plate. His disgusted, tight-lipped frown matched his stiff, knotted muscles and clenched fists. Mother was crying, a river of tears streaming down her pale, sunken cheeks, her eyes more bloodshot than I'd thought humanly possible. She tried to stifle her blubbering, but anguished whimpers and choked sobs burst out. She cracked an egg on the skillet, smashed it into pieces, threw it into the sink, and then reached for another egg as if it were the most arduous task in her life.

Horrified, I stared at my parents. *What had happened? Last night they'd been kissing …!*

The phone rang. No one reacted; my parents didn't even seem aware that it was ringing. Finally, on the forth ring, I lifted the receiver to my ear.

"What have you done?" Great Aunt Virginia's voice asked.

I stared at my parents, unable to talk without them overhearing. Suddenly I set the receiver onto the table, ran into my parent's room, pulled their phone off the hook, dashed back, hung up the phone in the living room, and then charged back into my parent's bedroom, slamming their door behind me.

"I'm sorry!" I whispered desperately into the phone. "I tried to help …!"

"It's wrong to use magic to compel others against their will," Great Aunt Virginia said. "I told you that."

"I know, but they were yelling …!"

"What was your chant?"

I thought hard.

"Make them love again,
Make them love.
Remember the good times,
Make them love."

A long silence followed.

"Fool child," Great Aunt Virginia scowled. "You've

tortured your parents."

"I didn't mean to!"

"Your parents have been having problems for some time, haven't they?" Great Aunt Virginia asked. "Serious, adult problems; did you do anything to resolve those problems? No, you threw them back together and forced them to remember their best times, but they couldn't forget the bad. When they awoke this morning, all of their problems seemed magnified, and now both are hurt and confused, uncertain what happened, and certain to blame each other since neither believes in ..."

"I can show them ...!"

"No, you can't!" Great Aunt Virginia warned. "They can't see it. They've closed their minds to Arcadia; all the tea in the world couldn't wash them into our land. Showing them things that they can't believe in threatens their sanity, especially in their current state."

"I'll take it back."

"Interfere again?" Great Aunt Virginia snapped. "Do you love your parents or not?"

"Yes ..."

"Then stop killing them," Great Aunt Virginia said. "Inanimate objects you can toy with, but every time that you toy with other people, you kill them, turn them into mindless automatons. Do you want your parents to become marionettes, dangling only on strings that you control? Because, once you grasp those strings, you can't ever let go. You'll spend the rest of your life manipulating every aspect of their lives just to keep them from realizing that they're not thinking anymore, simply obeying your commands. Your only hope after that will be to wipe their memories, not just in part: you can wipe away parts of their memories, but they'll notice that something's missing. You can supplant their bad memories with happy ones, but then they won't be your parents anymore; the individuals that they were ... you will have killed."

I burst into tears.

"What can I do?" I cried.

"Nothing," Great Aunt Virginia said. "I'll do what I can, but I can't fix the situation, and I won't remake your parents into mindless dolls. Stay away from them ... at least, for a while. Do nothing like this again."

With a curt good-bye, the receiver went dead. I stumbled back into my room, closed my door, and sobbed.

Hours later, Father opened my door. I sat up on my bed, still in the rumpled clothes that I'd slept in, and stared at him. He never spoke but looked sadly at me. He knelt down beside my bed, and we hugged long and tightly. Then, with an eerie silence, Father released me, stood up, and walked out of my room. I sat blinking, confused, until I heard the front door open and close. Then tears leaked slowly down my cheeks; *Father was gone.*

Twenty minutes later, Mother came in. She wasn't crying anymore, but her eyes were just as red, her pale expression vacant. She gave me the speech that I knew was coming: *it was just us now.* Father wasn't coming back. They were getting divorced.

Mother and I cried and held each other for a while, feeling both numb and helpless. Finally Mother dried her eyes and wandered back into her room. I sat powerless, feeling miserable and very responsible; *I'd been the straw that broke my parent's marriage.* I picked up my jump rope and hurled it across my room.

Soon, unable to sit and do nothing any longer, I opened my laptop and logged on. Hilary was online.

Audrey> Hi

Hilary> I'm grounded

Audrey> Sorry

Hilary> How did you do it?

Audrey> What did you see?

Hilary> HOW DID YOU DO IT?!?!?!?

Audrey> Exactly as you saw

Hilary> How?

Audrey> Poorly.

Hilary> You have to teach me

Audrey> It's dangerous

Hilary> Can I borrow the jump rope?

Audrey> Father left – divorcing mom – my fault

Hilary> They've been fighting for years

Audrey> I tried to fix them – their marriage – with the jump rope

Hilary> What?

Hilary> How?

Audrey> The jump rope caused it – I didn't know what I was doing

Hilary> I'll help – we'll be rich

Audrey> Great Aunt Virginia won't like that

Hilary> We'll give her a percentage

Audrey> She'll take back the jump rope

Hilary> What does she want?

Audrey> You wouldn't believe me

Hilary> Stay there – I'm coming over

Audrey> You're grounded

Hilary> Only if she catches me sneaking out

Half an hour passed before our doorbell rang. Mother came rushing out of her bedroom as I opened our front door, but it was only Hilary. Mother sighed heavily.

"Hello, Hilary. How's your mother?" Mother asked.

"She's fine, Mrs. Darby; a little shaken," Hilary said.

"Audrey can't leave the house," Mother said.

"That's okay," Hilary said. "We just want to talk."

"Audrey hasn't had lunch," Mother said. "Would you like a sandwich?"

"Yes, please."

Mother went into the kitchen. Hilary grabbed my arm and pulled me toward my room. There, she snatched my jump rope off the floor.

"How does it work?" Hilary demanded.

"I don't know," I said. "You just ... chant the chants ..."

"What chants?" Hilary asked.

"I don't know; I just make them up. Great Aunt Virginia knows, not me."

"Teach me."

"No, I ..."

Hilary flipped the jump rope open, gripping the handles.

"Not here!" I hissed, but Hilary ignored me.

With a mastery matching my own, Hilary began jump roping. I warned her to stop as my room shook with her bounces, the slaps of the rope like firecrackers exploding, but Hilary ignored me.

"What's going on in here?" Mother burst in through my door. "Jumping rope ... in the house?"

Hilary stopped under Mother's glare, and Mother looked at my jump rope in her hands.

"That's it, isn't it?" Mother demanded. "Aunt Virginia gave you that jump rope, didn't she? That's how you vanished from the mall. Give it to me." Hilary hesitated, but Mother stepped forward and yanked it from her hands. "I should've guessed; strange things always happen around Virginia. I wondered why your father sent you there ..."

"Mom, please!" I said desperately.

Mother stared at me and Hilary, and then at the jump rope in her hands.

"I ought to cut this up ..."

"No!" Hilary and I screamed.

"It's the jump rope," Mother seethed, staring at our terrified faces. "Why else would Aunt Virginia ...?"

"It's not hers," I interrupted.

Mother paused, staring doubtfully.

"Great Aunt Virginia was given it ... by ... Grandma Annie," I finished.

"No!" Mother said aghast, and she shook her head, staring at the jump rope as if it were a coiled snake. "What ... what ... does it ... do?"

"I'm ... not sure that it ... has limits," I said.

Mother considered, and then her expression hardened.

"You're never to touch this again," Mother said, shaking my jump rope at me. "You're forbidden to ever speak to Aunt Virginia ever again. Do you understand me?"

I stared, my mouth agape, but Mother didn't wait for an answer. She took the jump rope away and closed my door behind her.

Stunned, Hilary and I stared at each other; we'd just lost everything.

I told Hilary everything; there was no point keeping it secret now. Only her witnessing my vanishing from the mall bathroom made her believe any of it. I made her swear never to tell anyone, but I felt a dozen misgivings twist my stomach even as she promised to keep my secrets to her grave. I couldn't keep quiet; *I'd lost Father and Great Aunt Virginia all in one day.* All that Hilary cared about was losing the jump rope, but she became very interested in Great Aunt Virginia's tea set as well. I showed her the dresses that Great Aunt Virginia had given me, but she only scoffed and asked if people ever really wore stuff like that, and then she tried to find a label inside of them, and looked shocked when I suggested that they were probably hand-made.

Our phone rang, and a minute later, Mother came back in.

"Your mother's on her way," Mother said to Hilary. "Apparently you were grounded ...?"

Hilary bowed her head.

"I don't know what's gotten into you two," Mother said. "You both better shape up or you won't be seeing each other ..."

Mother's voice choked as she noticed the dresses.

"Where did those ...?"

"They're just old dresses, mom, nothing else," I said urgently. "Please, I won't even wear them ..."

"Give them to me!" Mother shouted, and she yanked them from my hands. "Vanish from supervision to God-knows-where, hide things, disobey … you're grounded for a year!"

Mother stormed out again, this time taking my dresses, and she slammed my door so hard that our whole building shook.

"We're in trouble," Hilary said.

"I'm not in trouble; I'm dead," I said. "If only I hadn't used the jump rope …!"

"We've got to get it back," Hilary said.

I shook my head; for all I knew, Mother might've already severed it.

Hilary's mother arrived on schedule. She apologized to Mother, who apologized back, and they were barely out our door before Hilary's punishments were loudly declared, starting with no TV or computer. Hilary pointlessly whined that these punishments were 'excessive' as Mother closed our door behind them. Then Mother turned to me.

"Did you know that Hilary was grounded?"

"Yes." Better that I didn't lie.

Mother locked our doorknob and the deadbolt.

"You're not to leave this apartment without me," Mother said. "You're never to leave my sight. If I go to the bathroom, you're to stand outside the door, and I expect to hear you talking the whole time. No TV. No computer. And no talking back."

Hours later, Mother relented enough to let me go to

my room. She didn't take my laptop or TV, but she promised that I'd never see either again if she came in and found either on. I had to leave my door open so that she could see me. I wandered about my big room, simpering, dejected, looking at all my fancy toys and wishing with all my heart that I was back in Great Aunt Virginia's tiny bedroom with her ancient stuffed animals and porcelain figurines.

Bored, anxious, I crawled through my closet, searching, and finally found my stuffed animals packed into an old box marked DVD player. I pulled them out, feeling very sorry; somewhere in Arcadia, these dolls were wandering about, forlorn, unloved. I stared at each of them, my old bear, my skunk with the padded Valentine's Day heart, and my white Pegasus with golden wings. I kept digging and found many that I'd forgotten: a green bird, a purple dragon, and a yellow and brown puppy with missing button eyes. Was he blind in Arcadia? I prayed not, and I determined to repair him, if I could. I didn't know where to buy doll eyes, but they couldn't be hard to find. In the back of my closet, crammed into the corner atop my shelf, I found a big pink frog that Father had won for me at a carnival six years before. I pulled it out as well and arranged all of them on my bed. Their blank eyes stared sightlessly, but I couldn't help but feel that I'd mistreated them. I hadn't purposed to hurt anything, but would I accept such an excuse after being boxed in a closet?

Mother came to my door and startled, seeing my stuffed animals laid out on my bed.

"No!" Mother said flatly. "I won't have it … not my daughter!"

Mother collected my stuffed animals in her arms and took them out of my room.

She didn't say a word to me all through dinner and spoke only to order me to put on my pajamas before bedtime.

The next day, Mother took me with her to work. She gave me a book, Modern Investing, and told me to read it during the day. I scanned it briefly, didn't understand a word of it, and sat bored as she answered phones and wrote project plans. We ate lunch at a nice diner, which she said we wouldn't be able to do again until the divorce was final, and then she let me Bing on her computer while she attended meetings. As I expected, Hilary wasn't online. We drove home in a hurry although no one would be there to meet us.

As we drove past the front of our building and turned into the parking lot, I spied a long, black limousine parked before our main entrance, and my eyes blazed. Upstairs, Mother pushed her key into our lock and her expression paled; our door swung open easily. Inside, sitting on our sofa, was Great Aunt Virginia.

Great Aunt Virginia looked austerely calm, her

every chrome-colored hair, every fluff of white lace, and the black ruffles of her long skirt exactly as they should be, save that she looked very out-of-place when not surrounded by antique dolls and tea cups. I wanted to cheer, but feared what Mother would say. Mother stared as if doubting her senses.

"I don't suppose you'll tell me how you got inside a locked door ...?" Mother asked.

"I'll tell you whatever you want to hear," Great Aunt Virginia said.

Mother grabbed me tightly and pulled me into the room, not letting go of my arm.

"*You can't have my daughter!*" Mother hissed.

"*Have?*" Great Aunt Virginia asked, shocked. "*Charlotte, you can't think ...!*"

"Jack left," Mother said. "We're getting a divorce."

Great Aunt Virginia closed her eyes and bowed slightly.

"Charlotte, I'm very sorry," Great Aunt Virginia said. "Jack was a good man ... in his own way. If there's anything that I can do ..."

"Why are you here?" Mother demanded.

"To talk," Great Aunt Virginia said. "I heard that you were going through a difficult time; I thought I'd save you the trouble of cooking."

Mother and I glanced at the kitchen, surprised to see two large, unfamiliar pots on our stove. Our table was set, complete with a bouquet of fresh baby roses.

"I want answers," Mother said. "I want to know how Jack put Audrey on a train and didn't remember. I want to know how Audrey vanished from a mall for four hours without anyone seeing her ..."

"Very well," Great Aunt Virginia said. "Perhaps you'd best ... sit down."

Mother sat in a chair, and then sent me to my room, but Great Aunt Virginia asked if I could stay.

"If I'm to tell everything, then you'll both want to hear," Great Aunt Virginia said, and she waved for me to stay. "It all begins with Great Grandma Annie. She was married at fourteen to a much older man, a very rich man, but also a very cruel man. Annie's Great Aunt Agatha gave her a child's tea set for a wedding present; everyone thought that it was intended for her children, but it wasn't. Great Aunt Agatha promised Annie that, as long as she believed, her tea set would let her escape whenever her hardships grew too great.

"Divorce being unthinkable in those days, Great Aunt Annie was forced to endure whatever her cruel husband doled out. To escape, she played with her tea set ..."

"Your tea set," Mother interjected.

"Our tea set," Great Aunt Virginia said. "Great Grandma Agatha said that it came from England, a birthday present to a princess, given to our family almost three hundred years ago. Twelve generations of our family have possessed it; Great Grandma Agatha gave it to Grandma Annie, who gave it to me. I'm giving it to Audrey."

My eyes flew open and Mother glanced worriedly at me.

"None of this answers my questions," Mother said.

Great Aunt Virginia smiled softly.

"Some explanations take time," Great Aunt Virginia said. "I can explain, but I can't make you believe. If I tell you now, will you believe?"

Great Aunt Virginia rose and walked into our kitchen. She lifted each pot's lid, dipped in a long wooden spoon, and stirred. Seeming satisfied, Great Aunt Virginia fetched our plates from the table, one at a time, and covered each with brown rice and a strange, tomato-rich stew from the pots on the stove. Steam rose from each plate as she set them back on the table. Then she opened the refrigerator and drew from it a glass pitcher that I'd never seen before filled with a light brown drink: iced tea.

As we ate, Great Aunt Virginia spoke up.

"Charlotte, my difficulty in explaining everything to you is that you can't believe. You've seen Jack have memory problems only when dealing with me. You've heard strange stories about me all your life. You could explain any of it, but you can't ... because you won't believe your own rationales. How am I supposed to convince you of things in which you refuse to believe?"

Mother paused, staring, but gave no answer.

"I needed Audrey; a man's life depended on her," Great Aunt Virginia said. "It'll never happen again. Audrey's learned what she needed to know. If you wish to learn what Audrey knows, then you must try to believe."

"Believe what?" Mother asked impatiently.

Great Aunt Virginia's frown deepened slightly.

"Where is the divide between reality and play?" Great Aunt Virginia asked. "Little girls play with dolls. Young ladies play with suitors. Grown women play with their husbands; to many people, life is a game, and their life is the playing of that game. Games mature as players grow older, but few adults grow wiser. What I need to prove to you is that play is just as real as what you call normalcy. Are you prepared to consider the possibility that I'm right?"

"Play is ... a waste of time," Mother said.

"Play is as important as happiness," Great Aunt Virginia said. "You can live without being happy, but why would you want to? Adult games are still games; play lightens hearts the same way that reality burdens: to be truly happy, you need balance."

Great Aunt Virginia reached out and carefully slid her hands over the bouquet of flowers in the tiny glass vase, just brushing their closed, dark red petals.

"Baby roses," Great Aunt Virginia said. "Do you like roses?"

"Very much," Mother said.

"Look at these; what do you see?" Great Aunt Virginia said.

Mother glanced at the roses but said nothing.

"See these pretty little buds? So young; they haven't opened yet."

"They're cut; they'll be dead before they open."

"Really?"

Great Aunt Virginia looked at the roses in their glass vase and smiled brightly. Slowly she passed her hand over them again as if lovingly caressing each with her light touch. Then she drew back her hand: every tiny rose bud had bloomed, fully and brightly.

Mother startled, staring at the tiny, suddenly-opened red blossoms, each petal spread wide. I glanced fearfully at Mother; I wasn't surprised at all, but how would Mother react?

"Say nothing," Great Aunt Virginia insisted, her eyes on Mother. "No words, no questions; believing takes time."

We finished our meal in silence. I wanted to reach out and see if I could make the buds close again, but I feared that Mother might freak out if she saw me do anything like that. Mother ate the whole rest of her dinner staring at the roses. She bent low and examined the cut stems submersed in water, seeking some mechanism to explain what had to be a trick. I said nothing; it was a trick, but Mother didn't believe in tricks.

I dried the dishes while Great Aunt Virginia washed. We had a dishwasher, but Great Aunt Virginia didn't trust machines to tell her when dishes were fully cleaned. Mother watched us the whole time, but snuck back and felt inside the rose bouquet, checking to make sure that there were no hidden devices. When we were done, we retired to the living room, where I sat beside Great Aunt Virginia on the couch.

"I have to leave," Great Aunt Virginia said. "I have a dear friend, a very wealthy gentleman, who lends me his car and driver. He's very kind, and I wouldn't wish to abuse his generosity by keeping his driver awake all night.

"Charlotte, you asked for an explanation: roses bloom to the sun because the sun loves them, and they love the sun. I also love roses, and I pray that they love me. That's how I got the roses to bloom. I didn't force them; I loved them. Love is real, like the love you have for Audrey, a powerful love that I would never interfere with. All that I've done to Audrey is open her eyes, far more than yours may ever open, to possibilities that growing up makes impossible. I ask that you don't question her tonight; think on what you've seen. Convince yourself that it never happened, if you wish. But, please, don't deny Audrey the chance for a happiness that you gave up on long ago."

Great Aunt Virginia rose and lifted a large leather

satchel. Around each of her pots, even around the pitcher of tea and the long spoon, Great Aunt Virginia wrapped a separate towel that she pulled out of her leather satchel, and then she squeezed everything back inside the satchel. After she buckled it closed, she set it beside the door, kissed Mother and I on our foreheads, thanked us for allowing her to visit, and voiced a hint that she'd gladly return, if it pleased us. With a blessing for our health and happiness, Great Aunt Virginia picked up her satchel and I held the door open for her. As Great Aunt Virginia departed with a stern, warning glare at me, Mother stood wordless, staring at me as if I were a stranger.

Chapter 8

Doll Houses

"Did you really save a man's life?" Mother asked as we drove to her job the next morning.

"I ... think so," I answered hesitantly.

"Do ... do you want to ... live with ... Aunt Virginia?"

"*No!*" I said forcefully, shocked that she'd even asked, and a few moments passed before I could speak again. "I just ... want to see her ... occasionally."

Mother stared out at the morning traffic and didn't look at me again.

That night Mother brought me the jump rope. She placed it in my hands and then stared at me. I swallowed hard.

"T-thank you," I whispered, and I started to turn away.

"Where do you think you're going?" Mother

snapped angrily. "You're not leaving my sight with that."

"Mother, I can't ..."

"So ... you'll show Aunt Virginia, but you won't show your mother?"

"I didn't show her, she showed me," I said. "She also said that it'd be dangerous to show you anything: dangerous for you."

"Why?" Mother demanded. "She showed me the roses ..."

"And did you believe?" I asked.

"Believe what?"

"If you believed, then you wouldn't ask," I said. "If I show you what Great Aunt Virginia taught me, what will it do to you? If you see anything, will you accept it? Will you want to learn to jump rope? Hilary does; she didn't believe at first, and now she wants me to teach her everything, but she'd abuse it. She'd hurt people and steal from them; I can tell. I'm afraid to show her anything."

Mother stared, her eyes drilling into me.

"What do you want me to do?" Mother asked. "Stay out of your life, not notice when my only daughter goes missing, not care if you're in danger ...?"

"I want you to trust me, mom," I said, and with a great sigh, I followed Great Aunt Virginia's example. "Tomorrow night ... after dinner ... I'll tell you everything."

"Why tomorrow?"

"Because ... today ... you won't believe."

"Everything?" Mother asked doubtfully.

"Everything," I promised.

Mother stood up, then paused and looked at me.

"At your age, I jump-roped every day."

Before work the next day, Mother gave me back my dresses, but she glared at me warningly.

"I expect you to be here when I get back," Mother said pointedly.

"I'll be here," I promised, holding my jump rope so that she could clearly see it ... so that she knew I wasn't lying.

I put on the paisley dress, then hiked up my skirt and put on jeans and a t-shirt to hide it. From my living room, I jump-roped to the familiar alley and ran up the cement steps to Great Aunt Virginia's, glad that no boys were gathered there at this early hour. A balding man with a briefcase was exiting the building, so I slipped past him, inside the security door, and ran up the stairs. Outside her door, I pulled off my concealing jeans and t-shirt, and then I knocked.

Several minutes passed before the door opened. Great Aunt Virginia appeared in a thick pink quilted robe, her chrome hair disheveled for the first time that I'd ever seen. She smiled when she saw me, but her eyes betrayed her weariness.

"Are you alright?" I asked.

"Yes, but I'm not ready," Great Aunt Virginia said. "Come in; I'll make tea."

"I'll make it," I offered, afraid that the effort would weaken her further.

Great Aunt Virginia sat in her kitchen and rested while I made tea. She let me pick my own recipe, but I asked for her advice several times. Again I used a lot of mint, but I also added mulberry twigs.

"Were you in Arcadia?" I asked.

"Yesterday was a difficult day," Great Aunt Virginia said. "We marched a long ways to the places where the other tin soldiers had vanished. You were right; at each location we found glitter."

"Glitter," I repeated, thinking, but unable to explain it. "When are we going ...?"

"We must go back today," Great Aunt Virginia said. "We have an appointment."

"Appointment?" I asked.

"Yes; they see no one without an appointment."

I wanted to ask who, but Great Aunt Virginia seemed very tired, so I told her all about Mother and what had happened, and apologized again for abusing the jump rope. After tea, at which Great Aunt Virginia and I shared biscuits and jam, I busied myself about her apartment, examining everything with intense curiosity, and even spoke a few kind greetings to the counterparts of Hiram, Muskay, and Princess Gracely sitting in their little chairs before the magic tea set.

More than an hour after I arrived, Great Aunt Virginia emerged from her bedroom perfectly coutured, every silver hair in place, her black silk dress spotless and unwrinkled. She stopped beside her front door and took her ebony cane, which bore its tiny eye-like red gems, and then she sat on her couch before the tea set. I had the tea hot and ready; I poured for five, complementing each doll and Great Aunt Virginia in turn.

"You may want to remain standing," Great Aunt Virginia said to me, and she stood with little effort, as if her grooming had strengthened her, and we drank the tea.

Arcadia appeared around us, but the sky was dark with low, gray clouds, and a brisk wind was blowing. We stood at the base of a great stone cliff between its rock wall and a row of thick hedges that seemed to have been planted just to shield this spot from view. A great cave opened in the high rock wall, its mouth ten feet tall. Directly over the mouth of the cave was a huge, wooden-framed window built right into the rock-face of the cliff. Just inside of the cave stood Hiram, Muskay, Princess Gracely, and Falcon.

I hugged each of them tightly, glad to see them after Mother's reluctance to let me return.

"What are we doing here?" I asked.

"Paperwork," Muskay said quickly with a

derisive sneer.

"We need information," Hiram said, "and it's best to gain knowledge at its source."

"Let's go in before we're late," Princess Gracely said.

"I hope that you can see in the dark," Muskay said to me.

"Ignore him," Falcon said, and he led the way inside the huge cave.

Never before had I been in a real cave. I'd always considered them fanciful oddities that only people in fairy stories visited, and I cautiously brushed my fingers against its rough stone walls just to prove that it was real. It was unexpectedly cold inside, even near its mouth. Not far inside, just out of the daylight, a pink-painted wooden wall blocked our path from floor to ceiling. Many huge flowers were painted on the wall, no two the same, and three white doors stood in the wall. The biggest door reached almost to the ceiling and was twice as wide as Hiram. The second appeared to be a normal door, and the last was so small that only tiny dolls could use it. On each door, reverently painted in silver and gold, was a fancy pair of scissors.

Falcon entered through the middle-sized door and Princess Gracely rushed us through as if every second that the door remained open was dangerous.

Inside the door was a vast office building, just like Mother's office would look if one outer wall was removed and each floor was only one foot high. Tiny desks sat in rows in each room, little stairs slanted between the floors, and the back wall seemed to be a huge filing cabinet with dozens of tiny drawers on every floor. It was oddly dark for an office; the only light came from the ceiling, where an odd assortment of mirrors were arranged all over, reflecting the sunlight from the window above the mouth of the cave into every corner of the many offices. On each level, small figures were working, a lot of them very busily, some hurrying about, but hard to see in the dim light.

A small woman with blonde hair and a smiling face approached us, and when she bowed to Great Aunt Virginia, the top half of her body seemed to vanish. I gasped; this woman was made of paper, just a picture of a woman, a flat, two-dimensional paper doll. I startled; she was so realistically-drawn that she could've been a photograph. I'd mistaken her for having depth.

"You're two minutes early," the paper doll said.

"We apologize," Princess Gracely curtsied to the tiny paper doll. "We don't mean to disrupt your important schedule."

The doll glared imprudently at Princess Gracely, then started to speak, when suddenly another paper doll ran up to her carrying a small slip of paper.

"Madame Paprus! Forgive me, but they said that this was urgent!"

The little girl had red hair and seemed to be drawn of crayon, not realistic at all, but her mismatched eyes succeeded in looking very worried.

"Excuse me," Madame Paprus said to us, and she snatched the small slip of paper from the crayon-girl's hand. She examined it for a moment, then handed it back and spoke in a crisp, sharp tone. "This should've been filed yesterday. Make ten copies and set one on my desk."

"Yes, Madame Paprus," the crayon-doll said, and suddenly she flipped open and became two identical paper dolls, connected at her hands and feet. She did this again; the crayon-doll was many layers of paper, tightly folded, until she expanded into six, eight, ten copies of herself. All were identical to the first, and they all ran off, clutching the slip of paper, toward a small, shadowed room with a 'Copy' sign over it.

"What's the paperwork for?" I asked Muskay in a whisper, wondering why dolls needed a busy office.

"No one knows," Muskay whispered back, "but I hear that every office is like this."

I started to laugh, but Great Aunt Virginia laid a restraining hand on my shoulder.

"My apologies; I'm a very busy woman," Madame Paprus said. "How may I help you?"

"We're investigating the disappearances of the baby dolls and the three squads of tin soldiers," Great Aunt Virginia said. "In our investigating, we've found numerous traces of glitter. You track and manage all ordering and shipping; have there been any recent shipments of glitter?"

"Glitter?" Madame Paprus asked. "Of course there have: we get constant demands for glitter, along with requests for marionette strings, hair-replacement yarn, plastic joints, and tin-polish. We never get enough tin polish."

"Could you tell us who ordered the glitter and where it was delivered?"

"Is it important?" Madame Paprus asked huffily. "I have many demands on my time."

"Very important," Princess Gracely answered.

"Arcadia is facing a new threat," Hiram said.

"Yes," Muskay said. "What a pity it would be if a beast with a thousand clawed tentacles were to break through your biggest door."

Madame Paprus startled, but Great Aunt Virginia spoke up.

"We don't know that such a threat exists ..."

"It almost killed me!" Falcon objected.

"... but we are investigating," Great Aunt Virginia continued. "We hope to avert another catastrophe."

"Please do," Madame Paprus said, and she turned and walked away, speaking over her shoulder. "Please wait here; I'll locate the invoice."

She walked away into the dim offices where she spoke to several other paper dolls, all of whom instantly turned and rushed off.

"Paper dolls are Arcadia's most vulnerable inhabitants," Falcon said to me. "They have to live in this cave: a single raindrop can warp them, and the slightest breeze can blow them away."

"Who built this?" I asked, looking about. "Paper dolls didn't make those doors."

"The hand-puppets," Falcon said. "They're our strongest and sturdiest allies, and as you'd expect, they're very handy. They love building things."

"It's sad," Princess Gracely said. "Paper dolls seldom get to enjoy sunshine and warmth."

"Good thing that they keep so busy; it must warm them," Muskay said, grinning. "Maybe a nice, big fireplace ...!"

Falcon, Princess Gracely, Hiram, and Great Aunt Virginia glared at Muskay so fiercely that he fell silent and never finished his joke.

Madame Paprus came back out of the shadows carrying a slip of paper in each hand.

"You're lucky," Madame Paprus said. "Another shipment has just arrived, glitter and sequins, and the order forms were still on my secretary's desk."

"Where did they go?" Great Aunt Virginia asked.

"Who ordered them?" Hiram asked at the same moment.

Madame Paprus examined both documents carefully.

"The glitter was sent to the rag dolls," Madame Paprus said. "They received two pounds each of eight different colors only three days ago. They've yet to return the required receipt for delivery; I'll have to ... send someone to get it." Madame Paprus said this last bit very solemnly, as if ordering a death-sentence.

"We can deliver that message," Falcon spoke up.

"Indeed? That's very generous," Madame Paprus said, and she looked highly relieved. "The glitter was ordered by ... oh, my!"

"What is it?" Princess Gracely asked.

"This form isn't complete!" Madame Paprus said, and she looked shocked and angry. "There's no return address; how dare they process this? Heads will fold, I promise you!"

"Nothing ...?" Falcon asked.

"Only a name," Madame Paprus said. "The glitter was ordered by a Mr. Percival Unch." Madame Paprus turned and screamed so loudly that all movement ceased and every paper doll looked down, even from the highest level of offices. "Who is Mr. Percival Unch?"

Percival Unch was a name that no one had ever heard of, and after twenty minutes of a hundred paper dolls frantically searching through every file cabinet, and countless piles of stacked papers, no further details were revealed. Many requests were found, all ordered by the mysterious Mr. Percival Unch, but none listed any reference or contact information. None of the shipments were sent to him; all were delivered to well-known doll villages, so they'd been processed as usual, without delay. One order of sequins was delivered to a hollow tree, and Madame Paprus glared as she read its invoice.

"I'll order an immediate investigation," Madame Paprus growled softly, her paper edges almost crisping from her red-faced anger.

"I'm sure that you'll uncover the problem," Princess Gracely said.

"Unless you are the problem ...," Muskay chided, but Hiram elbowed him in the ribs.

"We must leave, I'm afraid," Great Aunt Virginia said. "We've little time and much to do before we fade."

"Thank you for visiting, and I hope that you return during happier times; not during work hours, of course," Madame Paprus said.

We left through the normal door; Muskay reached for the huge doorknob on the biggest door, but Princess Gracely scolded him.

"That much wind will blow all the paper dolls in circles, not to mention their piles of paperwork," Princess Gracely said firmly.

"As little work as they get done, it won't matter much," Muskay said, and Hiram opened the normal-sized door and pushed him out.

"We need to visit the rag dolls," Great Aunt Virginia said. "Audrey, we'll need you to get us there; it's a long way from here."

"The rag dolls?" I asked.

"I'll teach you the chant, but we should do it outside," Great Aunt Virginia said.

The glow of the jump rope grew, its sparkles glittering in the sunlight. I watched as it flipped past my eyes; the tall bushes and cave mouth faded with each pass of the rope.

"Concentrate!" Great Aunt Virginia said. "We all need to go."

I returned my focus to my chant, my jumps, and the rhythmic timing of my jump rope's slaps upon the ground. The sparkling sphere strengthened and expanded. I was succeeding; if only I could keep going. I noticed how the better I jumped rope the stronger the magic seemed. I used to know a lot of trick-jumps: the Irish Fling, the Wounded Duck, and the Behind the Back Cross, but I concentrated on what Great Aunt Virginia had told me to do and didn't try anything fancy. After what I'd done to my parents, I didn't want to blow anything else. Thinking of them, my heart sank, and my glowing sphere began to contract.

"What're you doing?" Great Aunt Virginia cried. "Focus!"

I pushed, forcing thoughts of my parent's aside; I'd deal with them later. I chanted louder, jumped faster, and my sphere of light grew, its edge passing over Hiram, Muskay, Princess Gracely, and Falcon, as well as Great Aunt Virginia. I pushed harder, determined to prove myself. The strain was growing, but I hardened my will and refused to give in. Then, suddenly, the resistance faded and jumping became easy again.

"Audrey, stop!" Great Aunt Virgina said. "Enough; we've arrived."

I slowed my rope, and then added a Single Side-Swing as a dramatic flourish to end my spell. Hiram, Muskay, Princess Gracely, and Falcon all stared, and then began to applaud. Great Aunt Virginia looked shocked.

"What was that?" Great Aunt Virginia asked, staring at me.

"J-just a trick," I stammered, worried that she'd be angry.

"Trick?" Great Aunt Virginia asked.

"Sure," I said. "I know lots of tricks. Jump rope has its own Olympics, you know."

"Olympics ...?" Princess Gracely asked.

"The Olympics, the greatest sports challenge, every four years," I explained. "You can see it on the Web."

"Web?" Falcon asked incredulously. "Spiders ... jump rope?"

"Spiders have eight legs, but they can't hold a rope ...," Muskay said.

"No, the Web ... online ... computers," I began, but from their expressions I realized that they knew less about computers than Great Aunt Virginia. "Nevermind. There are girls and boys who compete at jump rope before judges who are world-class experts, and the best jumpers win medals."

"Medals?" Princess Gracely asked. "Like the medals that General Walnut wears?"

"Exactly; it's a great honor," I said. "Each girl and boy represents their country, and they compete to see who's the best at jump rope."

"You'll have to show me these 'tricks'," Great Aunt Virginia said cautiously, "but not now; we've important work to do."

I glanced about; we were in another small town, like the military fort of the tin soldiers, but this was an old world village of charming cottages and shops. Dozens of small dolls stopped to look at us; these were cloth dolls, some of which were identical; I recognized them from TV commercials that aired only before Christmas. All were soft, cloth-sewn, some with yarn hair, others more realistic, and a few looked handmade. Some had faces painted on hard ceramic, or plastic heads over soft bodies, while others had faces made by needlepoint, masterfully-sewn. One was crude and lopsided; a child must've made it, but, I suspected, at one time, that this was someone's most-beloved doll.

"Good ladies, please go about your business," Princess Gracely said to them. "We've come to speak to Mistress Flax."

Hesitantly the rag dolls hurried on. We strode into the center of a crossroads. Their tiny buildings made me feel like a giant, though I was short compared to Hiram, who practically filled one street. The largest building, a shop with three floors, barely reached to my elbows, but they were all charming, large, fancy doll houses, each meticulously made, and I wondered what Mother would say if she found one of these in my bedroom.

"Be very careful not to step on anyone ... or bump into a building," Great Aunt Virginia said to all of us, though she mostly glanced at Hiram. "Come, let's find Mistress Flax."

We walked three blocks, which took only a dozen steps, and stopped before the largest building, a great rectangular structure with a wide balcony on its top-most floor. I glanced in through the rectangular, wood-framed windows; the building was full of rag dolls of countless shapes and sizes all busy working strange, wide, wooden machines. These machines were great moving frames that held countless spools of thread, and each clacked loudly as they lifted and lowered a wide, thin webbing. Long bolts of cloth were coming out of the back side of each machine. On equally wide tables, other dolls were treating the fabrics with sparkling colors.

"Look at that!" I exclaimed.

"They're looms," Great Aunt Virginia explained, "machines for weaving threads into cloth."

"I know that," I said. "Look at the tables, at what

they're putting on the cloth: glitter!"

Everyone bent low, amazed, and many dolls startled and stopped working, suddenly seeing our huge faces peering into their high windows. A few screamed and we backed off, lest we cause a panic. Less than a minute later, an old but masterfully-stitched rag doll emerged onto the balcony before us, coming out of the door in a great huff. She was made of cream-colored silk and her face was both stitching and paint; her lips sewn with bright red thread and her eyes were tiny green stitches, while her cheeks were pinked like faded red stains.

"Mistress Flax, you look lovely!" Princess Gracely said as she curtsied.

"A pleasure to see you again, Princess," Mistress Flax said. "I trust that you have a reason for disrupting my workers; we have a very tight deadline."

"That's why we've come," Great Aunt Virginia said. "We need to know who ordered all of the fabric with glitter."

"Who ordered ...?" Mistress Flax asked, appalled. "Why?"

"Another threat has come to Arcadia," Hiram spoke up. "Dolls are missing. Some have died."

"We found glitter at all three locations where dolls have vanished ... and where I was attacked," Falcon said.

"Unless you're responsible for the

disappearances ...," Muskay challenged.

"Muskay!" Princess Gracely scolded. "I'm sure that Mistress Flax isn't behind any threat!"

"We never meant to imply so," Great Aunt Virginia said to Mistress Flax.

"Have you ever heard of Percival Unch?" I asked.

Mistress Flax startled, then looked at me.

"How do you know that name?" Mistress Flax demanded. "Who are you? What kind of doll ...?"

"Mistress Flax, this is my Great Niece Audrey," Great Aunt Virginia introduced us.

"A pleasure to meet you," I said, attempting a curtsey such as Princess Gracely performed.

"A new jumper!" Mistress Flax gasped. "Welcome, Mistress Audrey. Welcome indeed!"

Mistress Flax performed a curtsey far deeper than anyone with bones could; she was pure cloth inside.

"Thank you," I said.

"We learned of the name Percival Unch from the paper dolls," Hiram said.

"Yes, but they couldn't tell us who he was ... or where he lived," Muskay sneered.

"Please help us," Princess Gracely pleaded. "Our need is desperate."

"I'll tell you all that I know," Mistress Flax said, "but I fear it won't help; our instructions are to deliver all orders of Percival Unch to the hollow tree just a mile south of here, where it will be picked up. We do as requested, and the bolts are always gone the next day."

"You've never met Percival Unch?" Great Aunt Virginia asked. "You never asked who picked up your fabrics?"

"No," Mistress Flax said. "No more than the hand puppets."

"The hand puppets?" Great Aunt Virginia asked.

"Yes, they're filling orders as fast as us," Mistress Flax said.

"What kind of orders?"

"I've never seen them," Mistress Flax said. "Strange chemicals, I understand, but I don't know what they're for. The hand puppets mix and prepare them, and then deliver them to a small cave, from which they vanish."

"How do the orders arrive?" I asked, daring to speak. "I mean, do they send letters?"

"Yes, by letter, but no one's ever seen who delivers them," Mistress Flax said. "They only appear late at night; they leave the letters tucked into my bedroom window."

"Your window?" Hiram asked. "Do you live on the ground floor?"

"No, I live on the second floor," Mistress Flax said. "I wake up in the middle of the night and the envelope is always there."

"The messenger must be tall to deliver the envelope," Hiram said. "Few dolls are that tall."

"How do you know when a letter has arrived?"

I asked. "What makes you wake up?"

"Oh, they always make a soft sound when they leave an envelope, just enough to wake me up," Mistress Flax said.

"What kind of sound?" Falcon asked, growing slightly pale.

"A buzzing," she said.

Everyone exchanged glances, and Falcon paled.

"What?" Mistress Flax asked. "Is ... buzzing... important?"

"Falcon was attacked, and almost died, out in the Aging Forest," Princess Gracely said.

"How horrible!" Mistress Flax exclaimed.

"Somewhat," Muskay said, leering at Falcon. "The important thing is, whatever attacked him ... buzzed loudly."

"Very loudly," Falcon said.

"That couldn't be my buzzing," Mistress Flax said. "Mine is soft; no one else has ever heard it."

"Very strange," Great Aunt Virginia said.

"Perhaps it buzzes louder when it attacks," Hiram suggested.

"What should we do?" Mistress Flax asked. "Should we stop delivery ...? Miss our deadline ...?"

"Certainly not," Great Aunt Virginia said. "Mr. Percival Unch hasn't harmed any rag dolls that we know of, and we don't want to alarm him, or let him know that we're searching for him." Great Aunt Virginia paused and looked thoughtful, and then she turned to me.

"Audrey, this may all come down to you; what do you suggest?"

"I think that we should find out what the hand puppets are making," I said, "and then we should stake out these delivery points; if we could identify the messengers, perhaps they'll lead us to their source."

"That sounds exceedingly dangerous," Falcon warned.

"I agree with Audrey," Hiram said.

"Falcon's right," Muskay jokingly argued. "Let's wait until this monster with a thousand claws comes after us."

"Don't be silly," Princess Gracely said. "Whatever's happening, we must face it before any more disappearances occur."

"We'd best keep going," Great Aunt Virginia said. "Let's get out of the village so that Audrey has room to jump."

"Mistress Flax, thank you very much for all of your help," Princess Gracely said.

"Anything I can do," Mistress Flax said, but she looked very shaken.

"Until we know what we are dealing with, the less that you tell the other dolls about this, the better," Great Aunt Virginia said to Mistress Flax.

"Of course, of course," Mistress Flax said, quite flustered.

We left Mistress Flax on her balcony and

threaded our way through the narrow streets, careful not to bump into roofs or step on the busy inhabitants rushing about. We reached the outskirts of the village a minute later, Princess Gracely holding Hiram's hand to steady him as he stepped awkwardly around the buildings without a trace of her grace.

"As long as we're here, maybe we should have a look at that hollow tree," Hiram said.

"An excellent idea," Muskay said as Falcon paled even more.

"We can't, not today," Great Aunt Virginia said. "Audrey has to get back; she has responsibilities in our world, too."

"We hope we're not taking too much of your time," Princess Gracely said to me. "We appreciate your help and don't want to cause you any trouble."

"No trouble," I said, though I suddenly remembered that Mother would be coming back from work soon ... and I had to be home before she arrived.

"We need to visit the hand puppets," Great Aunt Virginia said.

Soon I was jumping and chanting the charm that Great Aunt Virginia had hurriedly taught me.

Traveling by jump rope was the same as before, but this time the strain seemed greater, or perhaps I was just tired from our first trip, from the paper doll's cave to the rag doll's village. It took longer to form the sphere and greater concentration to expand it, and I found myself sweating and gasping before the gold and silver sparkles stretched to encircle all of us. By the time that the strain relaxed, I felt dizzy and a little sick, exhausted and unsteady. Hiram grabbed and supported me when I faltered and stumbled over my jump rope.

To my amazement, we arrived beside a full-sized building bigger than any I'd seen since coming to Arcadia. It was a wooden structure, very solid, and had only small, high windows far overhead, so high that I couldn't see inside. A great noise came from it; hammering, the grinding-scrapes of saws cutting wood, and many loud bangs and clatters. Great Aunt Virginia led us around the corner of the building where I saw another doll village not far away, but these houses were larger and more modern than the charming old-world doll houses of the rag dolls. Some of these buildings looked like miniature sky scrapers, and others were as ornate as cathedrals.

Through a thick door, we entered the large building; it was a workshop, mostly a carpentry shop, but it had a fire-blazing forge against the far wall, where molten metal was being poured into clay molds. Working inside the building were many hand puppets of countless varieties, both men and women, each shaped so that a human hand could fit inside them. I'd played with hand puppets a few times, but never like this; these puppets were wielding woodworking tools as if human hands gripped them ... with all the strength of real humans. Hammers drove nails and pegs into many wooden devices, including a new loom, some doll-sized beds and tables, and an almost-finished large cart-borne stage, like the ones that the marionettes danced in, but there were other projects in various states of construction that I couldn't recognize. The air was full of sawdust and paint fumes.

A loud steam whistle blew suddenly, and all the workers paused and looked up.

"Break!" shouted a hand puppet with a metal construction hat and a painted face, and he waved at all the workers. "No noise; we have visitors!"

"Boss Fist," Princess Gracely curtsied deeply. "A pleasure to see you again."

Boss Fist swept off his metal hat and bowed low.

"Princess Gracely, you're as lovely as ever," Boss Fist said. "Welcome, all of you, most of all Chief Sorceress Virginia the Bold."

"Chief sorceress ...?" I whispered, but Great Aunt Virginia cast a stern glare at me.

"So nice to see you, Boss Fist, and what impressive work you all seem to be doing!" Princess Gracely said. "You are truly the finest craftsmen ever."

At these words, a general murmur of approval whispered through the great workshop, and all of the hand puppets looked very pleased. Boss Fist beamed a wide smile.

"Mine's a great crew," Boss Fist said loudly, turning to make sure that all of his workers heard him. "You should see what we have planned ..."

"Forgive me, Boss Fist, but time presses and our needs are of the utmost urgency," Great Aunt Virginia interrupted. "A new threat has arrived, and it may take all our efforts to save Arcadia."

"We're at your service," Boss Fist said, and another murmur, more serious, ran through the workshop. "What do you need? A house? Furniture?"

"First, we need to see anything ordered by Mr. Percival Unch," Great Aunt Virginia said.

Boss Fist's smile instantly vanished. Many hand puppets exchanged worried glances.

"Problem ...?" Muskay asked.

"N-no, it-it's just ... he's our best customer," Boss Fist said. "He pays well, always in advance."

"Have you ever seen him?" Hiram asked.

"Well, no," Boss Fist said, "but I'm sure that he's a decent guy. We delivered fifty cribs to him just in the last few weeks."

"Fifty cribs?" Great Aunt Virginia gasped as Princess Gracely stifled a high-pitched scream. "That must mean ... why else would he want cribs?"

"The missing baby dolls!" Falcon exclaimed. "Mr. Percival Unch has the babies!"

"What ...?" Boss Fist demanded. "What about the babies?"

"They're missing," Great Aunt Virginia said. "They've been gone for almost a year."

"That explains why they stopped requesting repairs," Boss Fist said slowly, scratching his chin with a hand that looked like the thumb-sleeve for a glove. "They used to be regular clients; everything had to be child-proofed."

"Show us what you're making for him now," Hiram said.

Boss Fist led us across the workshop to a large back table where three candles were burning under a small iron cauldron, which was suspended by a metal stand. Inside the pot bubbled some heated white liquid, and many large bowls were laid out in order, each filled with some colorful mixture, mostly reds and pinks, but some greens, blues, and violets. Beside them, holding spoons and mortars, stood several very nervous hand puppets. Most of their mixtures sparkled.

"What are these?" Great Aunt Virginia asked.

"No idea," Boss Fist said. "The order form listed the ingredients and mixing instructions; we've been slaving over them for months. Very difficult mixtures, unusual ingredients; we've been working overtime to procure them."

"What's cooking?" Princess Gracely asked, peering into the slow-boiling cauldron.

"That's wax," Boss Fist said, shaking his head. "It had to be strained and bleached to remove its yellow color, and the bees weren't happy to give it up."

"What do they make?" Falcon asked. "I mean, in what form do you deliver ...?"

"Like this," Boss Fist picked up a long, thin, red pole and held it for us to examine. "Others are just fine powders and smelly oils."

Princess Gracely took the tiny red pole, which was no thicker than a toothpick, and five inches long. She examined it closely as it left red marks on her fingers.

"This is wax," she said slowly. "Very soft wax."

"Can't imagine what it's for," Boss Fist said. "We got our first request for it months ago, and the orders have tripled since then."

"What kind of smelly oils?" Muskay asked.

"Flower oils, mostly," Boss Fist said. "I've been sending out workers every week to gather roses, violets, and several herbs."

"This gets stranger by the minute," Falcon said.

"We also make these," Boss Fist said, and he lifted up a tiny piece of wood.

Great Aunt Virginia took this; it was oak, no more than an inch long, rectangular on one end, with a tiny handle on the other.

"What is it?" I asked, also looking closely.

"We don't know," Boss Fist said. "We've made a hundred of them; they're a pain to drill."

"Drill?" Great Aunt Virginia asked.

"Yes; if you look closely, there's thirty tiny holes drilled into one side, three rows of ten, each exactly halfway through the wood."

"A hundred of these ...?" Muskay asked doubtfully.

"And an order for another hundred just arrived," Boss Fist added.

"Do you know anyone who's met Percival Unch?" Muskay demanded.

"I never asked," Boss Fist shrugged.

"We can't worry about that now," Great Aunt Virginia said. "We need to depart. We've got more clues than we know what to do with, but nothing to tie them all together. We need to plan our next move. Take care, and don't take any risks. Audrey and I will be back when we can."

"Safe journey to you," Princess Gracely said.

Great Aunt Virginia turned to face me.

"If we don't leave now then you'll be late," Great Aunt Virginia said to me. "Are you ready?"

I glanced around the workshop, at Boss Fist, and at Hiram, Muskay, Princess Gracely, and Falcon, and then I nodded silently. Great Aunt Virginia closed her eyes and the large workshop of the hand-puppets started to fade.

Chapter 9

Preparing For Battle

Back in her front parlor, Great Aunt Virginia seemed unusually troubled.

"Organized deceptions are alarming," Great Aunt Virginia said as she set her ebony cane to rest against the arm of her couch. "Mr. Percival Unch has taken great pains to conceal his doings; that implies that there may be other trickery that we haven't uncovered. Oh, look at the time; your mother will be home soon."

Quickly she took me downstairs; the older boys were lazing on her doorstep, but at one glare from Great Aunt Virginia, they quickly got up and slunk away. Great Aunt Virginia followed me into the alley, kissed me, and stood guard as I jump-roped away.

Mother arrived only a few minutes later, which allowed me just enough time to change out of my dress into modern clothes. She bustled in, said hello, and rattled on about one of her coworkers trying to impose incorrect standards on all of her weekly reports. Then she hurried about the kitchen, noting that we needed groceries, and that I should play in my bedroom until supper. I obliged her; we both knew that she didn't want to talk until she had time to focus. I paced about my room, too anxious to lie on my bed, waiting; I was still officially grounded. Without my computer, TV, or my stuffed animals, my room seemed cold and uncomfortable.

After a mostly-silent dinner, Mother sat tensely, still drinking her diet soda, when I spoke up.

"I'm ready to tell you everything."

Mother said nothing but plied her whole attention on me. Hesitantly I described my first meeting with Great Aunt Virginia on the train platform and how she'd whisked me to her apartment and showed me how to make tea. Although I tried to look elsewhere, I noticed that Mother's eyes widened as I explained how I poured tea for Hiram, Muskay, and Princess Gracely as they sat before the magic tea set. By the time I described how I'd used the jump rope to heal Falcon, Mother's eyes flared.

"That's enough!" Mother snapped. "Do expect me to believe ...?"

"No, I don't," I said, struggling to remain calm. "Arcadia has to be experienced."

"And I can't visit there?"

"I wish that you could," I said. "I'd love to take you."

"She drugged you, didn't she?"

"Great Aunt Virginia doesn't use drugs ... and neither do I."

"Hypnosis ...?"

"Arcadia is real, or ... at least, when I'm there, it's as real as being here. I don't know why; if you can't accept that, then you can't get there."

"Dolls and tea sets; I thought you were too old ..."

"Great Aunt Virginia isn't young."

"Do you want to end up like her?"

"What's wrong with her?"

"She's different, odd, eccentric; people avoid her."

"What's wrong with being different?"

"Different is dangerous," Mother's voice lowered as if she were whispering a nasty secret. "People don't trust you. They exclude you and soon ... soon you're an outsider. I know ..."

"Know what?" I asked.

"I ... I used to be popular," Mother said in a secretive whisper. "In school, I was the center of attention, always invited to everything, and then I met your father. Some of my friends didn't like him, and I tried hard to force them together, always hoping that they'd become friends, but it didn't work. In the end, I had to choose; my friends ... or your father. My family didn't like him either; they had nothing in common with him. He was different, but when I chose him, I accepted his differences. It made me an outcast. Even now, I wouldn't go back and change it; we had many happy years together ... and a beautiful daughter that I couldn't live without, but I miss my old friends. I feel very lonely ... all the time."

Popular? I stared at Mother; *how could she ever have been popular?* She sounded like she'd once been a teenager, which I knew she must've been, but I couldn't picture it.

"I don't want you to be an outcast," Mother said. "You deserve a good life. I don't want you wasting your life with dolls and tea sets ..."

"I don't want that either," I said.

"Arcadia isn't real."

"Baby roses don't bloom when you touch them."

Mother winced as if punched.

"That ... was a coincidence," Mother said. "Some kind of trick ..."

"Or an inability to believe," I said.

"Audrey, you're a beautiful young girl," Mother said pleadingly. "The whole world is open to you; the real world. You can have ... and do ... and be anything that you want ..."

"As long as I'm not different?"

"You'll thank me someday," Mother said.

"Different isn't always bad," I said. "Presidents and Olympic athletes are different ... and people love them."

"So be a president, or an athlete, but don't become Aunt Virginia," Mother said. "In life, there are ten thousand roads that you can choose from, and no matter which road you choose, being different always travels the more-difficult road, and lessens the chance that you'll ever achieve any destination."

"I'm not you, Mother," I said. "I'm not trying to be popular."

"You should," Mother said. "Popularity opens as many doors as beauty."

"Meaning ... that I'm neither?" I asked, biting back my snarl.

"I never said that ..."

I glared at Mother, and then I got up and stormed into my room.

"Maybe you should have Hilary for a daughter!" I shouted just before I slammed my door.

The next morning, right after Mother left for work, the phone rang.

"Great Aunt Virginia!" I cried, delighted to hear her voice. "I was about to come there."

"That's why I called," Great Aunt Virginia said over the phone. "Mistress Flax is making a delivery of new, sparkly fabrics this evening. I need to rest. At midnight, I'll be leaving for Arcadia; we're going to watch from hiding and see who collects the goods."

"Can I come?" I asked.

"Audrey, midnight is way past your bedtime," Great Aunt Virginia said.

"You need me," I argued. "You may be facing the monster and I've got the jump rope ..."

"Impossible," Great Aunt Virginia said. "Unless your mother gives you permission ..."

I frowned deeply.

"We had a fight last night," I said.

"About me?"

"About Arcadia; she said that it isn't real."

"Quite a sensible outlook, considering that she has no proof that it exists," Great Aunt Virginia said. "I suppose that she mentioned me, but you're trying to spare my feelings ...?"

"Yes," I admitted. "She doesn't want me being different."

"Nonsense," Great Aunt Virginia said. "Everyone is different. The problem with adults is that they always want what's best for their kids, meaning that they want you to enjoy the life that they used to dream of for themselves."

"I don't think that Mother ever dreamed anything."

"Your mother wanted to be a professional cheerleader."

"Really?"

"Oh, yes," Great Aunt Virginia said. "She was a cheerleader in high school, and very proud of it. She loved being popular and having people watch her ..."

"Mother was a cheerleader?" I still couldn't believe it. "What ... what happened?"

"Life," Great Aunt Virginia said. "Reality and dreams often conflict; most people eventually have to choose one or the other. Only the very lucky, and those who work very hard, make a reality of their dreams. The rest ... well, they find new dreams; smaller dreams, they'd say, because adults always compare their new dreams to their old ones. It's all quite silly; if your mother had become a professional cheerleader, then she'd have never had you, and you would've been the dream that she always regretted missing out on."

"I don't want to fight with her," I said.

"Then talk to her," Great Aunt Virginia said. "Ask about what life she wants you to have ... and why she wanted that life so badly. You may be surprised to find out that she and you both want many of the same things."

After Great Aunt Virginia hung up, I stared at the familiar walls, our modern, boring pictures and furniture. Finally I phoned Hilary.

"Audrey?" Hilary gasped, and her voice fell to a whisper. "Thank God you called! I'm not allowed to call you."

"Hilary, is your mom home?" I asked.

"Yes," Hilary said. "Hold on; I'll tell her that

you're a survey ..."

"No," I said. "Ask her if she'll talk to me."

"Are you crazy?"

"Let me talk to her ... or I'm going to hang up."

Hilary didn't believe me, but I said good-bye and threatened to hang up, and after calling me a bunch of names, her mother's voice came on the phone.

"Yes, Audrey?" Her mother's tone was very sharp.

"Mrs. Martin, I'd like to apologize for what I did," I began, trying to be honest. "It was thoughtless and inexcusable. I'm sorry. It'll never happen again."

"Do you understand the unacceptable position that you put me in?" Hilary's mother asked. "The legal ramifications, the damage to my reputation ... and my nerves, if something had happened to you?"

"Yes, Mrs. Martin. I'm sorry."

"You should be," Hilary's mother said. "What can I do for you?"

"With your permission, I'd like to come over," I said. "I'd like to see Hilary."

"Hilary's grounded. I'm surprised you're not ..."

"A lot's been happening here; Father left and he's not coming back."

A brief pause met this pronouncement.

"If I let you come here, do you promise not to leave without my permission ...?"

"Of course," I promised.

Hilary's face beamed as she opened the door. First

she pulled me inside, then she hugged me, and then she shook me angrily, and finally she emitted a frustrating sigh and dragged me toward her bedroom. I let her pull me along the familiar route into her treasure trove; Hilary loved the color gold. Nothing that she owned was real gold; her bedspread, curtains, lamp, and half of her decorations were gold-colored. Most of her picture frames, of which she had many, shined with gold leaf. The closest thing that Hilary had to real gold were tiny plated earrings that she'd gotten for Christmas.

"Where's the jump rope?" Hilary asked.

"At home," I said, and she stuck out her lower lip.

"When are you going to teach me ...?"

"I'm not," I said flatly, and Hilary's eyebrows lowered.

"I thought we were friends!"

"What would you use it for?"

"Everything!"

"You can't. There are limitations ..."

"We can work around those."

"Hilary, shut up! If you interrupt me again, I'll go home."

Hilary fell silent, her brown eyes bulging.

"The jump rope is more powerful than I ever imagined," I said. "Too powerful; one mistake and you could destroy everything that you hoped to gain.

If anyone ever found out about it, then they'd take it from us, and we'd never see it again. You can't wish for a million dollars; someone will ask where it came from. They didn't believe your story about me vanishing from the mall bathroom; they're not going to let you keep an unexplained suitcase of money. You can't use magic directly on people: that's forbidden ... because it always backfires. We're only twelve, and the one thing that I've learned since getting the jump rope is that neither of us are as smart as we think we are."

I paused, wondering if Hilary was even listening to me.

"Are you through?" Hilary asked impudently.

"No," I said. "I'm not going to teach you to use the jump rope."

"Why not?"

"I'm going to introduce you to my Great Aunt Virginia," I said. "I don't know when, or how, but I will. If she thinks that you should learn, then I'll teach you everything ..."

"Why does she get to choose ...?"

"Because I'm not smart enough," I said. "Neither are you. She is."

Hilary stared, confused, as if she'd never imagined an adult being smarter than a child.

"What if ... she doesn't like me?" Hilary asked.

"Then she'll tell you why," I said. "But I don't want you to learn to use a jump rope here."

"I'm grounded," Hilary reminded me. "Where am I

supposed to learn ...?"

"In Arcadia," I said.

"You mean it?" Hilary's face exploded into her widest smile.

"I think its best," I said.

Very excited, Hilary started asking me all about Arcadia again, and I had a lot more to tell her. She constantly interrupted me with questions about the paper dolls, the rag dolls, and the hand puppets. I answered as best as I could, although I only knew a little. I shared her curiosity; who did the paper dolls place orders with? Could a marionette walk if its strings were cut? What happened to dolls that got damaged over there? I could answer none of these questions, but Hilary and I spent hours speculating over them.

Hilary's mother surprised us with fajitas for lunch, but soon we were closeted again, whispering about glitter, the missing tin soldiers, and the baby dolls. We turned on her laptop and searched the web for pictures of the dolls, many of which I'd seen alive and walking.

"Why steal baby dolls?" Hilary asked repeatedly. "They'd be useless and require a lot of care."

I was still trying to think of an answer when Hilary's mom informed me that I had to leave if I was going to get home before Mother. Hilary hugged me very tightly, and I thanked Hilary's mom and apologized to her again before I left.

On the way home, I passed three little girls, no more than seven, who were jumping rope on the sidewalk while a mother sat reading a magazine, keeping a parental eye on them. I smiled at the girls; if Great Aunt Virginia had gotten her way, then I'd have learned about Arcadia when I was that age. I wondered what they believed in, and what games they played, and what dreams filled their young minds as their jump ropes passed over their eyes. Did kids ever accidentally vanish into dream worlds like Arcadia? Great Aunt Virginia had said something about that, but exactly what I couldn't remember.

"Mother, you won't believe in magic unless you see it," I said as we finished dinner. "I want to show you magic, if I can, so that you know I'm not lying."

Mother stared at me warily.

"If this is some trick ...," Mother warned.

"I want to spend the night with Great Aunt Virginia," I said plainly. "You can lock the front door with me inside. I'll use the jump rope right in front of you, and if I don't vanish, then I'll admit that it's all a lie, but if I do ... teleport ... then you have to believe me."

"Why should I?" Mother asked. "What is it that you want?"

I stared at her dumbfounded.

"Mom, all I want is for you to believe me."

"Why do you have to leave?"

"If I tell you then you'll accuse me of lying again."

"Arcadia ... is just a game that Aunt Virginia taught you."

"Yes, it is," I agreed, "but where does the game begin and reality end? This way you'll see the truth, and it can't be a trick; roses can bloom without magic, but kids can't vanish into thin air without real magic."

"What if you do vanish; am I supposed to just sit here, not knowing where you are?" Mother asked.

"Today's Friday," I said. "If I vanish, I'll be with Great Aunt Virginia all night and come back before breakfast tomorrow morning."

"And if you can't?" Mother asked. "If I don't see any magic ...?"

"Then you can have the jump rope and I won't see Great Aunt Virginia anymore," I said.

I knew as the words escaped my lips that it was a mistake. I wasn't sure that magic would work in front of Mother, but I had to try; I couldn't bear being considered a liar by my own mother. Mother agreed, and we waited until nine o'clock.

At nine o'clock precisely, I emerged from my bedroom in the red dress with the white cuffs and collar, the jump rope in my hands. Mother startled when she saw me and took in the dress with dire contempt.

"You never wore dresses for me," Mother said.

"I will now," I said, and I stopped in the middle of the room before our wide black television screen. "Are you ready?"

Mother hesitated, then reached to the side table and lifted up a large pair of scissors.

"If this doesn't work, if I don't see evidence to prove your lies, then I'm going to cut that jump rope into threads," Mother warned. "That's the agreement, right?"

I nodded grimly.

"If this works, then I'll vanish," I said. "Don't worry about me; I'll be with Great Aunt Virginia, as safe as I can be, and I'll return in the morning."

I shortened the ends of the jump rope by wrapping them around my hands; our ceiling was too low and I didn't want to hit our furniture. Under Mother's angry glare, I dropped the middle of the rope to my feet, stepped over it, and started jumping.

"Great Aunt Virginia's house
Far away
To Great Aunt Virginia's house
I jump today.
Must go now
Can't say how.
To Great Aunt Virginia's house
I'm on my way!"

I'd invented the chant since dinner, knowing that I

had to get it right. I tried not to look at Mother as she glared. I tried to focus on my chant, my timing, and even the steps of my Double Bounces. I also tried not to shake the apartment; breaking things and annoying the neighbors wouldn't make Mother any happier. But no sparkles came. I jumped faster and concentrated harder, but no sparkles came.

"I think that's enough," Mother said.

I didn't stop. Something was wrong, making it not work. I was focusing hard, concentrating, but the magic wasn't coming; no tingle, no draining other than physical exertion and worry about the scissors in Mother's hand.

"Give me the jump rope," Mother said.

I couldn't stop, and I couldn't keep this up forever. Something was preventing the magic; was it Mother's presence, her closeness, or that she was a non-believer? I flipped my jump rope desperately, almost shouting my chant; I had to find the magic!

The magic is in the play.

Suddenly I slowed my rope and softened my chant; *Mother wasn't holding back the magic: I was.* I wasn't playing; I was trying to protect my jump rope and prove myself in the real world. I forced all thoughts of Mother from my mind. I ignored the threat of the scissors. I thought about Boss Fist, then remembered Madame Paprus, and smiled about the silly Nutcracker generals all banging their heads together. I thought about Muskay, Hiram, and Princess Gracely all waiting to greet me when I returned. A childish smile widened my lips.

Sparkles shined and glowed gold and silver from the flipping jump rope. Mother's face looked horrified, aghast and disbelieving. As I jumped, I changed my chant, making it up as I went.

"Don't worry, Mama
I'll be right back.
In the morning
I love you much."

The sparkles enveloped me entirely.

I recognized the sensation of the completed magic from the tingle it gave me, like the pull of a yo-yo when it reaches its string's limit and starts to return. I was back in the alley, but never had I seen it after dark; it looked stark and ominous. I hurried out, shocked to find even more teenage boys lounging around Great Aunt Virginia's door than ever before. I quickly stepped back into the alley; a twelve year old girl in a dress was no match for bored teenage boys. I stepped into the shadows and started jumping rope very quickly.

"Great Aunt Virginia
Come help me!
I can't get in
The door's not free!"

No sparkles came, but a moment later, Great Aunt Virginia's muffled scream came from above. A window opened and Great Aunt Virginia stuck her head out and shouted down at the startled boys.

"You stay there!" Great Aunt Virginia screamed. "Do you hear me? Just stay and wait!"

"Shut up, crazy-woman!" one of the boys shouted, and all of the others laughed.

I pressed my back against the brick wall, hoping to stay hidden in the shadows, and I listened. I could see some of the street; an occasional car as it rumbled past, an old and scarred lamp post, and the closed windows of apartments across the street. I wondered what Great Aunt Virginia was doing, and if I could use the jump rope to make the boys go away, when suddenly red and blue lights flashed across the cars and buildings outside of the alley.

"Audrey!" Great Aunt Virginia's voice called. "Audrey, come here!"

A police car, flashing its lights, was driving slowly up the street; I stepped out of the alley. A spotlight from the police car illuminated the front steps of Great Aunt Virginia's apartment building, and many of the boys raised their hands to shield their eyes from the light, some snarling profane curses. The police car approached cautiously, but I hurried right into the crowd of boys, some of whom were startled to see me slipping past them in the blinding glare. Great Aunt Virginia pushed her door open as I reached it and closed it firmly behind me. She wore a dressing robe and slippers, and I was never so happy to see her.

"Audrey, that wasn't safe!" Great Aunt Virginia scolded me as we climbed the stairs to her apartment. "Dreams don't shield us from reality; these streets are dangerous ... even for jumpers."

Chapter 10

Dangerous Clues

Arcadia appeared so dark and menacing that I didn't recognize it. Tree branches without leaves forked down like knife-points at Great Aunt Virginia and I, visible only in the misty starlight. We were standing in a low row, a weedy gulch, on the edge of a forest, peering out at a field dotted with towering trees. No wind blew, and the only sounds were the disturbing snaps and creaks of the deep forest behind us.

"We must be quiet," Great Aunt Virginia whispered to me.

Great Aunt Virginia lifted her cane, which I hadn't noticed that she'd brought with her. Its ebony shape was invisible in the night save for the shine of the stars on its polished surface. As she held her cane aloft, the two tiny red gems, like secretive eyes, glowed with a pale red light, then quickly dimmed.

The jingle of tiny bells, which I instantly recognized, answered. Three shapes rose from the shadows; Muskay, whose hat bore tiny bells, Hiram, and Princess Gracely. They approached and slid in beside us.

"That's the hollow tree," Hiram whispered, pointing at a wide tree out in the center of the field. "A dozen rag dolls dropped ten bolts of fabric inside it at sunset, and we've been watching it ever since."

"Waiting for the pick-up," Muskay said, and in his voice I heard his delighted grin.

We stared at the starlit tree, which was little different from the other trees, save that it was bigger.

"Where's Falcon?" I asked.

Muskay scowled.

"Our friend Falcon has elected to report our disappearance should we fail to return," Princess Gracely said.

"Hiding," Hiram sneered.

"Bravery isn't a quality that everyone espouses; that doesn't mean that they can't be wonderful in other respects." Great Aunt Virginia said. "But please be quiet; tonight, too much bravery can get us killed."

Hours crept by as we waited, muscles cramping because we couldn't move about much ... and had nothing to do but worry.

"Hey!" Muskay whispered finally. "Is it getting darker? What's happening to the stars?"

"Be silent!" Great Aunt Virginia whispered anxiously. "It's worse than I feared!"

Across the sky slid a great invisible curtain, seen only as it blocked out the stars. Slowly it grew from the horizon, cresting like a vast ocean wave until it passed over our heads. Thousands of stars winked out behind it, and as it continued to encompass the whole sky, utter darkness fell. Eyes became useless, and fear of the dark gripped me.

"Listen!" Princess Gracely whispered.

My vision blotted into inky blackness. I focused on my ears and detected a frightful sound; distant buzzing. Quickly it grew louder, and I thought that I glimpsed colored sparkles in the darkness, although I couldn't see their shapes. Like will-of-the-wisps, the colored sparkles flew toward the hollow tree, then around and around it, buzzing like bees. Each was a different color, though almost impossible to see.

Slowly, even louder than the buzzing, came the tramp of tiny feet. A line of more colored sparkles appeared on what had to be the far side of the clearing, moving across the ground. It flowed forward like flood-waters, pushing through the tall, rustling grass. Soft footfalls stepped in rhythm like a marching army; I strained to see, but no light, no stars, and no moon glowed. Like marching-water, the colored sparkles spread across the clearing, between the low weeds and grasses, and quickly surrounded the hollow tree like a giant Christmas tree skirt. Then, without warning, the flow reversed;

the colored sparkles on the ground retreated, and moved away from us, back in the direction from which they'd come. The low sparkles marched away just as slowly as they'd advanced, and then the flying sparkles flew off over them, quickly vanishing in the distance. When the colored sparkles on the ground finally vanished into the woods on the far side of the clearing, the light suddenly grew. The curtain shielding the stars drew back, exactly as it had come, and our clearing was revealed in bright starlight again, exactly as it had been.

"Let's go," Muskay said.

We emerged from our hiding place and crept toward the hollow tree. Muskay reached it first and examined its spacious interior.

"Empty," Muskay said.

"What a confounded nuisance!" Hiram exclaimed. "All night, keeping watch, and we saw nothing!"

"We saw something," Princess Gracely said. "We just don't know what it was."

"We don't know what took the bolts of cloth," Great Aunt Virginia said slowly, and she leaned heavily upon her cane as she spoke, "but only one type of doll can bring darkness even to the stars."

"No!" Hiram said as Princess Gracely gasped.

"What?" I asked.

"Shadow puppets?" Muskay asked, and for the first time, he sounded frightened.

"Shadow puppets," Great Aunt Virginia said. "Our greatest enemy has returned."

"Shadow puppets?" I asked. "You mean ... like shapes on the walls?"

"Yes," Great Aunt Virginia said. "Long ago, way before television, puppeteers erected wide curtains and waited for night to fall, then stood behind their curtain with a bright lantern, making fantastic shapes appear in shadows. Many performed violent, frightening stories. Shadow puppets can grow to any size, appear in any shadow, and vanish at will. Only bright light kills them, so they hide during the day and come out at night to continue the horror that they once inspired."

Hiram bowed his head at these words, and Princess Gracely began to cry.

"The last time that the shadow puppets attacked, half of the dolls in Arcadia were slain," Hiram said softly.

"What's 'television'?" Muskay asked.

Great Aunt Virginia ignored Muskay and stood very silent, thinking.

"It doesn't make sense," Great Aunt Virginia said at last. "Shadow puppets don't leave glitter or need cribs, so why would they take the baby dolls? The shadow puppets blocked out the starlight, but what carried away the bolts of fabric?"

None of us could answer. I bent down and brushed my hand through the starlit grass beneath the wide limbs of the hollow tree. When I lifted my hand and examined it, tiny flecks sparkled all over my palm and fingers. I looked up to see Muskay, Hiram, and Princess Gracely staring at me.

"They went that way," I said, nodding toward the direction in which the sparkles had vanished. "Let's follow them."

"We don't have to follow them," Hiram said. "There's only one destination that way; The Factory."

"Factory?" I asked.

"Once, long ago, a terrible enemy came making great promises," Princess Gracely said. "He promised to build a great Factory to manufacture spare parts, and form a repair facility for our oldest dolls, modern shelters for the paper dolls, and a schoolhouse for the trolls. Everyone rallied around him, and the hand puppets labored long to construct his Factory ..., but he lied. His Factory, we discovered, was built only to reproduce dolls of himself, which he planned to deliver to your world, the human world, to restore his own popularity. The tin soldiers marched against him when his treason was discovered, but by then, he had an army of his own dolls, and he was so powerful that no weapon could touch him."

"Who was he?" I asked.

"Punch," Muskay said. "Punch is one of the oldest and strongest dolls that ever lived. He's a monstrous evil, and I'm sorry to say that he clothes himself as a jester." Muskay paused and sniffed haughtily. "He was the toast of medieval Europe for centuries, the most-popular puppet ever, and he delights only in political satire and cruelty. He'd have conquered Arcadia, but he was stopped by the only force that no man can resist."

"What?" I asked.

"Not what: who," Princess Gracely said. "Punch had a wife named Judy, as old and powerful as he, and as Punch's forces defeated the tin soldiers, Judy snuck up from behind and attacked Punch. Their battle lasted many hours, but when it was done, Judy stood triumphant. Punch fled from her wrath into your world and was never seen again."

"Punch!" I exclaimed. "That's it! Mr. Percival Unch! That could be ... P. Unch!"

"Punch ... and the shadow puppets," Hiram said. "What an unholy alliance!"

"It's far worse," Great Aunt Virginia said. "Those sparkles in the darkness, and the cuts that almost killed Falcon, weren't caused by Punch or shadow puppets. If my dear great niece is correct, then we've identified two enemies which threaten Arcadia, but an unknown third enemy still waits to be revealed."

"Three mortal enemies?" Hiram asked. "How can we defeat three foes at once?"

We all turned and stared at the trees under which the flowing sparkles had vanished.

"We have to go home and rest," Great Aunt Virginia said to me. "When next we come, we must undertake the greatest danger of all: we must visit The Factory and see if it's occupied."

Hiram, Muskay, and Princess Gracely nodded in unhappy silence.

"What can we do?" Muskay asked.

"You need to find Judy," Great Aunt Virginia said. "Without her, even a jumper can't defeat Punch."

"We will," Princess Gracely promised.

Again, Great Aunt Virginia escorted me into the dark alley, even though the steps before her apartment were vacant. Dawn was lightening the sky, but the shadows between the buildings lay trapped in night. I jump-roped back into my living room to find Mother asleep on our couch, an empty coffee cup on the table beside her. As my last few jumps shook the floor, she startled awake.

I ran and hugged her tight, and she started crying, and soon I was crying, too.

"I'm sorry," I said, not knowing why.

"No, I'm sorry," Mother said. "I didn't believe ..."

"Why should you?" I asked. "Until I'd seen it ... experienced it ... I didn't believe."

"How ... how does it work?" Mother asked.

"I don't know," I answered truthfully. "The magic ... it's in the play; I don't understand a bit of it. Great Aunt Virginia does, and I'm sure she'd tell ..."

"Aunt Virginia?" Mother said, raining tears. "I ... I've lost you, haven't I?"

"No!" I insisted.

"I can't ... give you the things that she can," Mother

sobbed.

"I love Great Aunt Virginia," I said, "but she's not my mother."

"Where did you go?" Mother asked. "Tell me everything."

Mother made a wonderful breakfast and I told her everything about our stake-out of the hollow tree.

"I screamed when you vanished," Mother admitted, sitting beside me and staring into her poached eggs, which stared back. "At first, I couldn't believe my eyes, and then I grew angry, furious that you'd kept this from me, but even madder that ... this whole other reality exists ... and I never knew it. I felt cheated ... robbed of the life that I could've had. Then, as the hours passed, I realized that I was being selfish and mean; I've known Aunt Virginia all my life. She'd always been polite and kind to me, and I always shunned her because of all the things that my parents said about her. I'd robbed myself."

"I'm not sure that Arcadia is reality, so you couldn't have been robbed," I said. "It seems real, but it's more like a game; I wish that I could take you there."

"Could you try?" Mother asked.

"We'd best ask Great Aunt Virginia before we attempt anything like that," I said, unsure how Mother would take it. "It could be dangerous."

"When do you go back?" Mother asked.

"Tomorrow," I said. "Great Aunt Virginia needs to recover from staying awake all night. Besides, Muskay, Hiram, and Princess Gracely are searching for Judy."

"I'll take the day off of work," Mother said. "I'll drive you."

"You don't have to ..."

"I need to apologize to Aunt Virginia."

Mother returned my stuffed animals to me right after breakfast. We arranged them about our living room, making it slightly resemble Great Aunt Virginia's apartment. My old bear got the place of honor: center on the back of our couch. My skunk with the padded Valentine's Day heart sat happily under the table lamp, and my white Pegasus with golden wings we placed on our highest bookshelf from where he could fly all around the room. My green bird perched near the coffee pot in the kitchen, and my purple dragon presided over our television, in the position of highest power. My yellow and brown puppy we left on the table beside the baby roses; Mother knew where we could buy replacement button eyes and assured me that she'd sewn many new eyes onto her own dolls when she was a child. My big pink frog sat in the corner, as he was too big for the furniture.

"I don't even know what happened to my dolls," Mother said regretfully. "I left them at home when I went off to college, and then your grandparents turned my room into a large bathroom, and their little bathroom became a walk-in closet. When I went through their things I never found my dolls. They must've given them away ... or thrown them out."

"Gave them away, I hope," I said. "Maybe some other kids are loving them now."

Mother smiled wanly.

We went shopping that morning at a craft store that had a wide selection of large and small button eyes. Mother also found new jump ropes for sale; she bought me one *'in case I needed an extra'* and a second for herself, suggesting that she might try and see if she could still skip a few passes. That afternoon, after we returned and Mother sewed new eyes onto my yellow and brown puppy, I got tired of watching TV and opened my computer. To my amazement, Hilary was online.

Audrey> Aren't you grounded?

Hilary> Mother's out shopping. Do you have the jump rope?

Audrey> Yes

Hilary> Great!!!

Audrey> I demonstrated to Mother; she knows everything now

Hilary> What?!? I thought this was our secret!!!

Audrey> Mother's OK with it

Hilary> No way!

Audrey> She's driving me to Great Aunt Virginia's tomorrow

Hilary> Can I come?

Audrey> Not this time; we're going to The Factory

Hilary> Factory??

Audrey> I've got a lot to tell you.

Hilary> Can I come over?

Audrey> Mother's here; if you break grounding, she'll tell your mother

Hilary> Tell me what's happening!

Audrey> Not this way; call me on the phone.

Hilary and I spent hours on the phone that afternoon, and I told her everything, glad that we were still friends. She didn't ask if she could use my jump rope, but I knew that she wanted to. She wormed every detail out of me that she could, especially focusing on my jump rope chants; from the pauses in her voice, I suspected that she was writing them down.

Mother and I arrived at Great Aunt Virginia's house around 11 A.M. Some boys were lazing upon the steps, but they only sniggered as Mother dragged me past them. I was wearing the first dress that Great Aunt Virginia had given me; dark green with a black vest, laced up the front with white ribbons. The boys laughed at me, but I ignored them; if they had no class then that was their loss.

Great Aunt Virginia and Mother hugged long, and both looked teary, but Great Aunt Virginia recovered first.

"Nonsense," Great Aunt Virginia said. "My sister kept you as far away from me as she could. She had no tolerance for anything outside the ordinary; there was no way that her daughter was going to become friendly with me, not if she could help it."

Mother watched delighted as I made the tea, this time all by myself, and I ground it exceptionally fine. Great Aunt Virginia complemented me on my selections and attentiveness to my grinding, and let me pour the powdered tea into the boiling water. We had a very nice conversation while the tea steeped, and Mother asked many questions, but Great Aunt Virginia refused to answer most of them.

"Play, if you examine it too closely, ceases to become play," Great Aunt Virginia said. "Arcadia is real to Audrey and I, but we have to be careful; if our visits fail to remain play, then Arcadia will vanish for us, and we'll never be able to visit it again."

"I wish ... I could go there," Mother said.

"Perhaps someday, when you're older ... and ready to play again," Great Aunt Virginia said. "For now, it's enough that Audrey can visit; our need for a jumper has never been greater."

"Is ... is Arcadia dangerous?" Mother asked.

"Less dangerous than this world," Great Aunt Virginia said with a sorrowful sigh. "I can't say that dangers don't exist everywhere, but Audrey's young and clever; I'm sure that she'll be fine."

Great Aunt Virginia invited Mother to make

herself at home in her apartment, to help herself to the refrigerator and anything else that she wanted. Mother gave her and I a kiss before Great Aunt Virginia brought out the steaming teapot and set it on the table amid the miniature cups, plates, and saucers, which again looked like they'd just been washed. I poured for six, complementing Hiram on his manliness, Muskay on his wry slyness, and Princess Gracely on her eternal beauty. Mother sat on the chair and stared, wide-eyed, as I put down the teapot and sat beside Great Aunt Virginia on the couch. Great Aunt Virginia had her ebony cane leaning against her and I had my jump rope in my lap.

"We may be gone for some time," Great Aunt Virginia warned Mother.

"I'll be here when you get back," Mother promised.

We drank, and slowly our vision of Mother grew foggy, and then she was gone.

Chapter 11

The Mystery and the Trap

Hiram, Muskay, and Princess Gracely sat in chairs around the big table, which was now set in a clearing beside a flowering willow tree. In the distance came faint hammering sounds; we weren't far from the tiny, modern city of the hand puppets.

"Welcome again," Princess Gracely said, but her tone was depressed.

"What's wrong?" Great Aunt Virginia asked.

"We found where Judy is ...," Hiram said.

"But they won't go there," Muskay scowled.

"We can't," Princess Gracely said. "Judy's at ... The Palace."

"The Palace?" I asked.

"Then we must go there," Great Aunt Virginia said.

I could tell that Princess Gracely was deeply troubled by this pronouncement, and even Hiram seemed unsettled. Muskay alone smiled.

Seed, cinnamon, and chocolate-glazed cakes sat on the large plates of the pink and blue floral-patterned tea set, and Princess Gracely insisted that we have some to strengthen us on our journey. I ate excitedly; I'd only seen palaces in movies like Cinderella and Sleeping Beauty, and I was thrilled that I was finally going to see a real palace. Hiram and Princess Gracely's reluctance mystified me; *who wouldn't want to visit a palace?*

After tea, Great Aunt Virginia taught me the chant, and I happily jump-roped us all to The Palace. I was quite taken aback; The Palace wasn't gleaming white with a high, crenellated stone wall and tall towers streaming long red banners. The Palace was a grimy little shack, an old, two-story theater with a big sign that was encircled in gold-colored light bulbs, some of which were broken. Another faded red sign over the bulbs had 'The Palace' written in large swirling letters. It looked very grimy and run-down, shaded by overgrown trees whose long branches lay unkempt upon its sunken roof. Behind cracked glass, ornately-framed posters covered the front of its dirty walls, advertising live performances with very antique-styled drawings of jugglers, arm-in-arm dancing girls in knee-length skirts, and smiling men in tuxedos with top hats and canes. The marquee above the unlit ticket-taker's booth read 'The Amazing Arnold and Mr. Magee', and under it, in smaller letters, it read 'Ventriloquist Extraordinaire'.

"This is 'The Palace'?" I asked softly.

Muskay answered my question by pointing up at the

obvious sign on the front of the building. I shook my head and sighed; no Prince Charming was awaiting us inside this relic.

"It's said to be haunted," Princess Gracely whispered.

"Come," Great Aunt Virginia said. "Arcadia depends on us."

Great Aunt Virginia rapped on the old timbers of the wooden door with her ebony cane. The aged door creaked open, and she pushed inside. The Palace was dimly lit by tiny flames from small oil lamps burning in cob-webbed wall-sconces, which gave the air a humid, greasy smell. We entered a wide room where brass fountains behind a bar must've once dispensed popular drinks, and a big, dust-covered mirror stood behind the bar, dimly reflecting our images. The rest of the walls were covered in faded, blood-colored, felt-striped wallpaper, which was peeling in many places, upon which was hung more framed posters of actors who probably never lived to see the twenty-first century. Once, when clean and bright, this must've been a charming theater foyer, but disrepair and shadows loomed ominous and threatening.

Great Aunt Virginia led the way. We passed through creepy swinging wooden doors into the main chamber of an old-fashioned theater. Red-cushioned wooden seats sat in long rows, festooned in dust and cob webs, untouched for decades. The aisle led past two dozen long rows of chairs to a wide stage which was brightly-lit by more tiny oil lamps placed evenly around the front edge of the stage behind little shields, which prevented the lights from shining upon the two hundred empty chairs. Beyond the footlights, the stage was bare save for a single empty wooden chair in its very center. Dark red curtains hung on both sides of the stage, while a bright gold curtain hung behind it.

All that I could think of was that Falcon would never come here, and my own trepidation was growing. The Palace was eerily silent, yet screamed of delighted crowds and loud applause that only these ancient walls remembered.

Great Aunt Virginia led us through a narrow doorway beside the stage into the darkness of the very back. Old doors, some with five-pointed stars painted on them, lined a hallway lit only by the reflected light from the stage, which came down a tiny open doorway leading up a small flight of five steps. I peeked out at the empty stage as we passed the bright doorway; never had I seen a stage from this angle. Then we passed onward.

"Welcome," breathed a soft voice from the shadows. We all startled, then glanced about, uncertain of the strange voice's origin. "Here; this way."

We followed the voice up another short stairs, and found ourselves on the backstage, behind the golden curtain, which had many tiny holes that we couldn't see from its front, each streaming a thin ray of light through the otherwise dark chamber. We passed many ropes that were tied to wooden fixtures, each rope running straight up until it vanished in shadow; I could make out no ceiling, and suspected that it was very high. Many wooden crates were stacked behind the ropes, and then I saw a tall lamppost, but only the front half; a prop once used to decorate the stage. A great wooden heart stood behind it, surrounded by what looked like a grand doily, but it was only white-painted wicker bent into curling, decorative shapes. The backstage was littered in old props, and we threaded between them until we came to a great gold-painted throne which was mostly hidden in shadow. Upon the throne sat the largest doll that I'd seen in Arcadia, and as I watched, its ivory eyes opened.

"Welcome, my honored friends," the ventriloquist's dummy said, leaning forward so that a single spot of light streaming through the holey curtain illuminated his face. He was made of masterfully-carved wood, with moving eyes, with a mouth and ears that flapped on hinges, and his eyebrows raised and tilted from side to side. He wore a dusty black tuxedo made to fit him, and he had shockingly orange hair that was slicked back as if greased. He lifted a hand and waved us forward, and I noticed a stiff wire hanging from his wrist, such as a puppeteer might use to mimic life in his wooden dummy. This dummy, however, was very alive, deep and mysterious; no dummy at all.

Shivers ran up my spine as he stared at us from his shadowed throne; Princess Gracely clutched protectively on Hiram's thick arm.

"Mr. Magee, it is our honor," Great Aunt Virginia said, her voice discordant in the grave-like silence, where every sound was swallowed as if criminal. "Forgive our intrusion ..."

"No intrusion," Mr. Magee interrupted in his soft, wispy voice. "The doors of The Palace are always open to the jumper."

"We thank you for your kind hospitality," Great Aunt Virginia said, "but I'm the jumper no longer; please meet my Great Niece Audrey."

Mr. Magee swiveled his wooden head, and his ivory eyes, with their painted black pupils, rocked back and forth and finally settled on me.

"Great Niece Audrey, welcome to Arcadia ... and The Palace."

I swallowed hard, unable to speak, but I performed a deep curtsey as best I could. Great Aunt Virginia went on to introduce our friends, and Mr. Magee welcomed each of them.

"We come at a time of great need: Punch has returned to Arcadia," Great Aunt Virginia said.

"I know," Mr. Magee said slowly, as if ignoring her urgent tone.

"Punch has allied himself with the shadow puppets," Great Aunt Virginia said.

"I know," Mr. Magee repeated.

Great Aunt Virginia glanced at us, her shadowed face worried.

"Do you know what other threat Punch is allied with?" Great Aunt Virginia asked.

"Yes," Mr. Magee said slowly. "It is a terrible new threat, more powerful than both of the others combined. You can't defeat this enemy. If you try, and fail, then Arcadia will fall."

"There must be a way ...," Muskay said.

"Relics can't compete; the old fades, like The Palace, to make way for the new," Mr. Magee said.

"We came to find Judy ...," Muskay said.

Mr. Magee's eyebrows lowered to where they rested right atop his ivory eyes. The eyelids slowly closed, then reopened, as if blinking woodenly.

"Judy can't help anyone," Mr. Magee said. "Judy ... was taken away ... eighteen months ago."

"What?" Hiram gasped. "More than a year ago ...? That's before the baby dolls vanished."

"And the tin soldiers," Mr. Magee said slowly, turning to face Hiram. "I don't know what became of Judy or the tin soldiers, but the baby dolls are still alive."

"At The Factory?" Muskay asked.

"You've been investigating," Mr. Magee surmised, turning his wobbly eyes to face Muskay. "You can't rescue the baby dolls; the enemy holds them."

"Why?" Princess Gracely asked. "What could

they want ... with babies?"

Mr. Magee shook his wooden head, then looked at Princess Gracely.

"Babies have many uses to villains like Punch," Mr. Magee said. "The baby dolls labor to support Punch's new allies, the doom of Arcadia."

"What are these allies?" Great Aunt Virginia asked.

Mr. Magee glanced at Great Aunt Virginia, and then turned his eyes upon me.

"What I have seen I cannot name," Mr. Magee said softly, menacingly. "I know what I've witnessed, but I know of no name for them, and no name did they give. They took Judy, who was older, and far more powerful, than I, with little effort. I can say no more, save that Great Niece Audrey, our new jumper; she will know them, and name them, even if no other can."

I cringed, alarmed; *I would know them?* But Mr. Magee leaned back into the shadows of his golden throne.

"Thank you for coming, but I can help you no further," Mr. Magee's soft voice spoke from the darkness. "The Palace is my home, and if doom approaches, I shall meet it here, dying in the place where I lived. You are welcome to return anytime you wish; my performance begins nightly at eight."

Great Aunt Virginia thanked Mr. Magee repeatedly, and then we crept back through the spooky theater, into the dusty foyer, and out under the failing marquee. Outside of the shabby, crumbling Palace, we gathered in the golden rays, letting sunlight cleanse and warm our chilled limbs.

"I don't understand," I said. "How will I ...?"

"Mr. Magee was frightened," Princess Gracely said. "I didn't think that was possible."

"It bodes ill for us," Hiram said.

"Bah; Mr. Magee should help us, not hide in his ruin," Muskay said.

"Help can only come from those willing to fight," Great Aunt Virginia said. "We've done all that we can here. Now we must face our enemy at last; we must go to The Factory."

"But how can we hope to prevail?" Princess Gracely demanded. "An enemy greater than Punch and the shadow puppets ... and allied with both?"

"Prevail we must," Great Aunt Virginia said. "Come, Audrey; you must learn the proper chant. This time, precision matters."

I practiced until I could recite the chant flawlessly, as any variation could land us within sight of The Factory. I jump-roped all of us to a tiny glen inside an overgrown thicket.

"Perfect!" Great Aunt Virginia complimented me. "Audrey, you really are a champion jumper."

"No time for that, Virginia," Muskay said. "Every minute here is dangerous. Audrey, are you ready to get us out of here at a moment's notice?"

"Of course."

"Muskay, you're our sneakiest," Princess Gracely said. "Why don't you go spy, and then come back and report."

"Audrey has to go," Hiram said. "Mr. Magee said that only she would recognize our true enemy."

"I don't think that we should split up," Great Aunt Virginia said.

"The more eyes that look, the more chances we'll be spotted," Princess Gracely said.

"We'll need to crawl in some places," Muskay said.

"I'll go," I quickly offered. I loved Great Aunt Virginia, but I couldn't imagine her crawling on the ground at her age. "We'll take a peek and then hurry back."

"Very well," Great Aunt Virginia sighed with a reluctant frown.

With a nod at me, Muskay slowly slid into the thick leaves around us. I tied my jump rope about my waist and followed him, batting back the wire-like branches, shielding my eyes from their dangerous twigs. We had to duck low, and I was glad that I could do this for Great Aunt Virginia, to whom such a path would be a terrible hardship, although I would've preferred to be wearing my jeans instead of a dress. Then we lowered onto our hands and knees and crawled uphill through the thick bushes, trying not to loudly crunch the dried leaves and fallen branches. Our going was slow and difficult. We inched forward, unable to go faster. Finally Muskay slid to a halt, laid down on his chest under a ceiling of thick green leaves, and whispered for me to climb up beside him. We peered out together.

The Factory was a great rectangular gray-stone castle, a life-sized medieval fortress, and it had many chimneys, only one of which was belching smoke. It looked like a toy castle blown to adult size, but built of real stone, with turrets, battlements, and towers, but it seemed to be all one building, not a great hall surrounded by a thick wall. The Factory stood in a wide clearing right below the hill upon which we were hiding. No one seemed to be guarding its walls; except for the smoking chimney, it appeared to be deserted.

"Should we go closer?" I asked.

"No," Muskay said. "Shadow puppets can't come out in sunlight, but other things can. We need to see what we're facing, not risk our lives."

We laid there long, but nothing happened. Distant birds chirped and flew about, but none came near the castle, or The Factory, as they called it. Then we heard the deadly buzzing, just like we'd heard at the hollow tree.

"Crawl back," Muskay whispered urgently. "Hurry, before they find us."

"Just another moment," I said, grabbing his arm and looking about. "If I can just get a good look at them ..."

Suddenly Princess Gracely's scream drowned out the buzzing. Muskay and I glanced at each other, and then turned and tried to force our way back through the thick bushes, to scurry down the overgrown hill, but the countless branches barred rapid progress. Hiram's painful shout, followed by Great Aunt Virginia's horrified screech, joined Princess Gracely's screams.

"Stop!" Muskay shouted, pushing back against me. "Let's go around!"

Quickly we shoved our way back to the top of the hill and tore free of the clinging bushes, out from cover, into full view of The Factory. We darted along the bushy ridge to the right, seeking an opening in the foliage. Suddenly, just when we were about to plunge back into the woods, Hiram, Great Aunt Virginia, and Princess Gracely screamed behind us. They burst out of the woods from the other side, running down the hill toward The Factory. Flying things were chasing them; little women with wings. I gasped: *I recognized them instantly.*

"Glamour dolls!" I cried, and I started forward, but Muskay's arm seized me.

"What are they?" Muskay shouted as he pulled me back.

"Glamour dolls!" I said. "Hilary has dozens; they're fashion dress-up dolls! They can't harm ...!"

But just as I said it, a glamour doll with bright, flashing, violet fairy wings slashed past Hiram, who raised an arm to fend her off. A deep slice appeared on his forearm where the glamour doll had struck him, and I saw something silver gleam in the flying doll's hands.

"A scalpel!" I cried. "The glamour dolls have scalpels!"

A dozen winged glamour dolls burst from the trees and dove upon Hiram, Princess Gracely, and Great Aunt Virginia. I tried to run forward, but Muskay held me back.

"Use the jump rope!" Muskay shouted.

I'd forgotten, but I pulled out the jump rope free and began at once.

"Glamour dolls, glamour dolls,
go away!
Get away from my friends,
go today!"

It wasn't much of a chant, but I meant it with all of my heartfelt fury. However, just as I began to chant, the fairy glamour dolls stopped and looked at Muskay and I. After only an instant's hovering, four glamour dolls broke off and flew toward us, while the others continued savaging Hiram, who was using his huge body to shield Great Aunt Virginia and Princess Gracely, both of whom had fallen, blood trickling from shallow cuts on their faces.

A wave of light burst from my flipping jump rope, blasting back the winged fairy dolls. Three were knocked backwards, but one merely staggered, then flew forward. She was blonde, her tiny, thin, painted eyebrows knit in anger, a snarl on her plastic lips showing familiar plastic teeth that I'd never before seen gritted in angry determination. She looked exactly like Hilary's glamour dolls; inhumanly-perfect figure, long, unbending legs, thick hair bound in a pony tail, and a violet skirt that exactly matched her buzzing wings layered with heavily-glittered scraps of purple lace. She flew faster and more graceful than any bird, but no bird loomed as evilly.

The next revolution of my jump rope struck her, and knocked her down onto the grass. The violet glamour doll screamed in pain, and her gleaming silver scalpel fell from her hands, but she'd disrupted my swing; my jump rope faltered. I struggled to maintain its failed momentum and keep from tripping, but my magic instantly dissipated. The three fairies that had been blasted backwards zoomed forward, and the pink glamour doll, as she approached me, slashed her scalpel at my jump rope's thin cord. I screamed and tried to pull it away, but without need; the point where the pink glamour doll struck my jump rope sparked with magic, and she was encased in tiny electric-yellow streamers. She screamed and collapsed to the ground, her pink wings singed, her carefully-coutured black hair suddenly frizzy. But the green winged fairy didn't slash with her scalpel; she kicked at my jump rope, and this time its momentum caught and failed. I stumbled and almost fell, and the last fairy, with a light-blue dress and wings, buzzed swiftly past my cheek, and a shallow, stinging gash opened just below my eye.

Muskay cried out and jumped at the light-blue fairy, but instantly he drew back his hand, blood flowing from his palm. The violet glamour doll leapt into the air, buzzing her wings fiercely, and she grabbed the middle of my jump rope and pulled, as if she'd yank it from my grip. But I held tight; glamour dolls were small, thin, and plastic: no match for my strength. I yanked back and caught the violet fairy in one hand, drew back, and threw her away with all of my might. Far off she flew, but instantly she righted herself and zoomed back toward me.

Muskay cried out again, and Hiram's bellows echoed over the clearing. I saw him struggling to protect Great Aunt Virginia and Princess Gracely, raining blood as eight colorful fairies slashed at him with razor-sharp surgical instruments, flying rings around him and the women.

"No!" Princess Gracely screamed, and suddenly she raised both of her arms high into the air. Glass grew from her hands, like a giant sugar crystal forming in seconds. It enveloped them, and I recalled that the same huge crystal had once encased Falcon, and this time I realized what it was: a giant rhinestone. Her rhinestone-crystal expanded to encase Great Aunt Virginia, the badly-bleeding Hiram, and herself. All froze instantly, and the murderous flying fairies were driven back. They struck again, swinging their deadly scalpels at the transparent surface of the great rhinestone-crystal, but its clear solidity rebuffed their mightiest blows. The winged glamour dolls screamed, tiny, high-pitched wails of fury, and then they turned toward Muskay and I.

Muskay had picked up a thin, fallen branch and was swinging it at the violet, green, and light-blue winged fairies. They darted around his swipes, slashing, and dried leaves fell from his branch with every pass. I stepped over my fallen, slack jump rope, and tried to flip it over me again, but before my second pass, the violet fairy zipped away from Muskay and kicked my cord again.

"They won't let me jump rope!" I cried to Muskay.

"Keep trying!" Muskay said, and he jumped behind me as I flipped the rope again over my head. To my amazement, Muskay jumped with me as my rope hit the ground beneath us; team-jumping, which I hadn't done since I was six. He jumped well; only Princess Gracely was more coordinated than Muskay, and in-between our jumps, Muskay swung his branch. The violet fairy flew back, but the green fairy slipped up behind Muskay's back and kicked my jump rope's cord; again its momentum failed.

The other fairies arrived and dove at us. I screamed as twin gashes sliced through my thin sleeves. One fairy flew low, and a biting sting erupted from my calf. I quit trying to jump rope, instead swinging my jump rope like Muskay swung his branch, driving the fairies back.

"We've got to get out of here!" Muskay shouted.

"I can't jump rope with them interfering!" I shouted back. "Besides, we can't leave the others!"

"We've got no choice!" Muskay cried. "Look!"

Horror filled me as I glanced toward The Factory. Out of the castle gates marched a vast army of glamour dolls. Suddenly I realized what had flowed like sparkling water across the ground to the base of the hollow tree, and carried away the glittery fabrics that Mistress Flax and the rag dolls had stashed there for delivery: the sparkles had returned, but now I could clearly see the glitter, glass beads, sequins, and tiny colored rhinestones on their countless colorful dresses. Thousands of glamour dolls, without wings, came marching up the hill. Ten thousand, perhaps, marching in perfect unison, their tiny high heels making the strange sound that I'd heard in the darkness at the hollow tree. On their long plastic legs, the army of glamour dolls marched quickly through the green grass, the sun sparkling off their exotic, new-looking dresses and the huge colorful bows in their hair.

Looking at them, I screamed. The flying glamour dolls wouldn't let me use my jump rope, my only weapon, which I'd thought was invincible. Soon the ten thousand marching glamour dolls would swarm over us and bury us in plastic. They were small, but too many, and quickly approaching. If we tried to run then we'd end up like Falcon, sliced to pieces. If we stayed here, then we'd be overrun by twenty thousand spiky plastic high heels.

I stopped uselessly swatting at the fast-flying

winged fairies and reached down. The pink, black-haired fairy still lay upon the grass where she'd been magically-stunned after attempting to splice my jump rope with her scalpel. I scooped her up; her hard plastic body felt familiar in my hand, but her limbs hung unusually limp from her joints. The other fairies gasped and raised their bloody scalpels, but I held the unconscious pink fairy up before them, and with deliberate cruelty, I grabbed one of the many thin, pink, glitter-coated strips of fabric hanging from her tiny sewn waistband, and jerked it hard. The thin fabric ripped, and the flying fairies screamed, hovering staggered in midair. Even the marching glamour dolls froze instantly, staring up at me with utter revulsion masking their usually-sweet faces. I threw away the torn scrap, letting it sparkle in the sun as it fluttered to the ground. I flipped the pink fairy over, seized one tranquil wing, and gestured as if I meant to rip its translucent wing clean off.

"No!" Ten thousand glamour dolls screamed in perfect unison.

"Back off!" I shouted. "Leave us alone!"

All of the glamour dolls, the wingless dolls on the ground and the fairies flying just out of reach, spoke as one with ten thousand girly voices.

"Don't ruin her."

"Go back!" Muskay said. "Leave us in peace and we'll leave your companion whole."

"We can't," the glamour dolls said together. *"We are ordered to get you."*

"Who gave that order?" Muskay demanded.

"King Punch," the fairies and earthbound glamour dolls said.

"Bring your king out here," Muskay shouted. "If he dares face a jumper, let him come!"

The glamour dolls all exchanged glances, and then the flying fairies alone spoke.

"We must return for orders," the winged fairies said in unison. *"Wait here."*

As one, the winged fairies flew off, all but the unconscious pink fairy in my hands, their buzzing fairy wings flashing in the sunlight as they flew back toward the stone castle. The vast army of glamour dolls stood, some glaring at us, others looking frightened and confused.

"We should go," Muskay said. "We can outrun them."

"I can't leave Great Aunt Virginia!" I argued.

"There's no hope for them," Muskay said. "These dolls won't let us near them. Use your jump rope; you've got to go for help. I might not get another chance."

"You ...?" I asked, offended.

"You can escape anytime," Muskay said. "Just fade; go back to your world. You can then regroup and come back for us. Go now: once night falls, the shadow puppets will come out."

"You run; I'll hold them off," I said.

"Without your jump rope, I won't get far,"

Muskay said. "Too late; here they come!"

Out of the wide Factory doors, the colorful winged fairies slashed through the air in spiraling paths, the excessive glitter on their dresses leaving sparkling trails in the air behind them. I examined them closely as they came; each was a different color and fashion; the red fairy wore the shortest skirt, the midnight-blue fairy wore a deeply-plunged neckline, and her hem reached to her ankles, and the sparkling black fairy's tight skirt had the longest slit. Eleven winged glamour dolls flew up and hovered before us.

"We're commanded to bring you to King Punch," they said in unison.

Muskay and I exchanged glances of deep concern; *if we walked into The Factory, would we ever come out alive?*

Chapter 12

The Hopeless Parley

I'd always wanted to walk across a real castle's drawbridge, but as the wide doors of The Factory yawned before me, I was glad that no drawbridge existed; getting out of here would be hard enough. The flying fairies led our way, and the countless glamour dolls without wings marched behind us as escort. Some of the walking dolls carried scalpels like their flying cousins, enough that they posed a formidable threat. To my utter dismay, several thousand glamour dolls, as weak as they were individually, had lifted the giant rhinestone crystal in which Princess Gracely had encased herself, Hiram, and Great Aunt Virginia, and the glamour dolls carried them in behind us. Seeing them lift the heavy stone, my trepidation grew; Muskay and I pressed against each other, and I kept my jump rope and the unconscious pink fairy tight in one hand, my other firmly gripping her fragile wing.

Loud mechanical noises greeted us as we entered the foyer, a stone-flagged chamber lined with rooms whose inner doors were almost closed, but movements shifted in the utter darkness within the doors, and soft, wicked laughter wafted distantly from their shadows. We marched past these doors into a large, noisy chamber, and I gasped; the room was full of baby dolls: *the missing babies!* They sat in even rows upon the stone floor, and before each was a small table bearing a toy sewing machine. All of the babies were busy wielding scissors, cutting out little patterns of glittery fabric, or stitching all of the tiny pieces together on battery-powered sewing machines. *They were making dresses for the glamour dolls!* This was why the baby dolls had been stolen; *to labor in an underage sweatshop to make new fashions for their masters!*

I started to protest, but Muskay grabbed my arm and gestured warningly, and we crossed the sweatshop, following the flying fairies. Babies of all sizes and colors, swathed only in diapers, crawled or toddled about. Some babies were mixing colorful powders and potions, then dividing them into little containers; doll makeup, bright lipsticks, eye-shadows, and blushes. I gnashed my teeth in outrage. *These baby dolls were slaves!*

Other baby dolls were gluing tiny tufts of bristles into the inch-long rectangular wooden ends with the tiny handles that we'd seen Boss Fist and the hand puppets making: hundreds of tiny hair brushes for the glamour dolls.

Behind us, a thousand marching glamour dolls carried the giant rhinestone inside, Princess Gracely, Hiram, and Great Aunt Virginia encased in its crystal safety.

At the far end of the sweatshop, we entered a vast chamber so brightly pink that I winced to see it. Another noise met my eyes; a giant TV screen filled the back wall, but my attention was drawn by the countless slots on the wall, between the high, narrow windows, like endless little shelves, each just big enough for one glamour doll to lie down in. The slots reached from the floor to the ceiling, easily twenty thousand slots. Many of them were occupied, and the floor's flag-stones were mostly hidden by countless glamour dolls.

"Do you have perfect hair?" unseen speakers from the giant TV blared. "Is it silky, shiny, and manageable? Do away with split-ends and dull, lack-luster hair. Color-treat with ..."

The commercial cut away and another instantly began.

"Your smile is your greeting to the world. Are your teeth as white as they should be? You deserve dazzling, sparkling white teeth, the kind of smile that instantly attracts attention. Until now, only dentists could give you the kind of smile that everyone wants to see ..."

The teeth commercial ended and a tall, beautiful woman wrapped only in a towel filled the screen.

"Your skin needs to be soft and velvety ..."

I ignored the rest; at twelve years old, I'd already seen enough commercials to last a lifetime, but many of the glamour dolls were staring at the giant TV screen, completely mesmerized.

Suddenly a huge figure burst from the floor as if popping up on a giant spring, the world's largest Jack-in-the-Box. It was a doll, but it rose over eight feet tall with a huge head like a papier-mâché Mardi Gras mask. Big and red, he was dressed similar to Muskay's jester's outfit, but his garish garb was dark and menacing, not plush and amusing. Punch had massive wooden feet, like a giant marionette without strings, and in one hand he carried a huge wooden paddle such as might be used to row a canoe.

"Surprise!" Punch shouted, his high-pitched voice blasting distressingly over the noisy TV speakers, the buzz of the flying fairies, and the clatter of the babies' sewing machines. "Welcome to The Factory, my future for Arcadia!"

Punch's smile shined alarmingly big teeth at me, and his oval eyes glared evilly above an overly-large nose that seemed to weigh down his leering face. He had jet black hair, a thin moustache and beard, and thick eyebrows that seemed painted on, but which moved as his huge head bobbed forwards and back.

Without warning, Punch lifted his huge wooden boat-paddle and swung it at me. I screamed and threw up my arms. My jump rope, which I still held in one hand, met his wooden paddle like two mighty swords clanging together. With a loud ringing crash and a flash of magic, we were both driven back one step.

"A jumper!" Punch screamed as if cursing. "Drat! But you can't defeat me. Glamour dolls, kill them!"

Some of the countless dolls started forward, but I held up the unconscious pink fairy and grasped her wing tightly.

"No!" cried all the flying fairies in unison.

The advancing glamour dolls stopped, staring up at me.

"Where's Judy?" Muskay shouted suddenly.

"You!" Punch shouted, looking malevolently at Muskay. "I don't know this new jumper, but I remember you!"

"Your day is over, Punch," Muskay shouted.

"Miserable, second-rate jester!" Punch cursed.

"You disgrace the jester uniform!" Muskay shouted. "Kidnapping babies, making them slave for your minions ..."

"My new order shall make Arcadia greater than ever before," Punch screamed.

"Greater for who?" Muskay demanded. "For you and your mercenaries?"

"I'll tear the stuffing out of you, jester!" Punch cried, and he swung his paddle at Muskay.

"Swing!" Muskay cried as he jumped behind me, and I lashed my jump rope forward. As before, the plaited jump rope and wooden paddle collided with a loud metallic clang and a concussive flash that drove both of us back.

"You'll feel my fury soon enough," Punch seethed. "Even a jumper can't prevent the sunset. Once my shadow puppets arise, you'll both die."

"He's right," Muskay whispered. "Audrey, fade back to your world and come back with help."

"What about you?" I asked.

"I'll be fine, but trapped here," Muskay whispered. "Go!"

"No!" I hissed at him. "Not until I know that you're safe!"

"Very well, but the instant that I'm safe, you fade," Muskay said. "Get ready ... now!"

Suddenly Muskay sprang backwards, did a flip in midair, and landed flat across the top of the giant rhinestone crystal. Inside, Princess Gracely, Hiram, and Great Aunt Virginia never moved, being fully encased, but the crystal suddenly expanded. The giant rhinestone grew larger, fully encasing Muskay inside its protective crystal, and engulfing several dozen glamour dolls with him. Punch roared in anger ... and I screamed.

Punch swung again and I matched his attack, but his anger was so great that I was forced to retreat. The clangs of our battle resounded, the magical blasting driving back both us and the countless watching dolls. I gave way, backed up, and found myself facing a dark doorway opening upon a steep downward stairs. Punch was too big for this doorway; I threw the pink fairy at him and dashed through the narrow doorway, leaving him cursing behind me. Punch screamed in rage and struck his mighty paddle hard upon Muskay; the rhinestone crystal cracked; a hundred fractures appeared on its surface, but instantly it healed itself, becoming sparklingly clear. Muskay was unharmed, and Punch bellowed in fury.

I ran down the stairs, which ended only one flight below. A few candles illuminated the chamber downstairs, which was much smaller than the large room above, and it had many doors.

"Fade!" I shouted at myself, and only then did I realize that I had no idea how to fade. I'd done it many times, but never with the jump rope, only with Great Aunt Virginia; *I didn't know how to fade on my own.*

Evil laughter came from the darkness. Shadows grew and the dim candlelight seemed to waver and flicker. I was in the dungeon of The Factory, where, even in the daytime, the shadow puppets ruled. Dark shapes of long fingers and reaching arms rose upon the walls and floated across the floor toward me. This was my last moment; *I had to fade!*

A bright wooden gleam attracted my attention;

hanging from stout hooks, barring a closed door, was a paddle exactly like the one that Punch held, a barrier preventing the door from opening; *Judy must be trapped in that room!*

The shadow puppets reached me and the candlelight failed. Cold shivers and every terror that I'd ever known gripped me mercilessly. I was smothered, swallowed by darkness. The most horrible feeling of my life overwhelmed me, every fear that I'd ever had; I had to escape or go mad!

"Mother!" I cried.

Suddenly I faded. Grasping shadow-hands clawed in vain as Arcadia drifted away. Great Aunt Virginia's apartment appeared around me; I'd faded, escaped, but the others, even Great Aunt Virginia, were trapped in Punch's Factory by foes whom I could never hope to defeat.

"Audrey!" Mother cried. "What happened?"

Mother ran forward. She snatched up a white cloth napkin from the magic tea set and pressed the spotless cloth to my face. It stung, and when she pulled it away, I saw my blood staining the linen; I hated the sight of blood, especially my own, but greater needs pressed.

"They've got Great Aunt Virginia!" I shouted at Mother. "They got Princess Gracely, Muskay, and Hiram, too!"

"You need a bandage," Mother said. "Who's got them?"

"Punch! They're trapped at Punch's Factory!"

This statement needed considerable explanation, but it was some time before I could describe everything. I finished telling Mother what had happened in the kitchen where she brewed both of us some tea while I held the napkin pressed against my wound.

"I don't know what to do," I said to Mother as the tea steeped. "I've got to go back ..."

"You're not going back," Mother said.

"What?!?"

"You could've been killed!" Mother said. "Scalpels? One bad cut and you'd have bled to death! What kind of crazy woman is Aunt Virginia, taking you into such a dangerous place? That's it: no more Arcadia!"

"But what about Great Aunt Virginia?" I argued. "She's trapped ...!"

"She never should've gone in the first place," Mother snapped. "She knew what she was getting into ... what was she thinking? At her age? Come; we're leaving."

"Mom, we can't!" I shouted.

Mother turned to face me and held out her hand.

"Give me the jump rope," Mother said.

"No! Mom!"

"Now!"

Mother took the jump rope, grabbed a thick

pair of shears from Great Aunt Virginia's counter, and before I could stop her, Mother cut the magic jump rope in two. With a loud snip, the two halves separated and fell apart like dangling, useless dreams. I stared disbelieving; Mother had severed my only link to Arcadia, the only tool that could possibly save my friends.

"Nooooo!!!!!" I screamed, filling the whole apartment building with my rage, echoing out onto the street.

I shouted things at Mother that I'd only heard Father shout, nasty things so terrible that no lips should ever utter them. Furious, Mother slapped my face so hard that I fell, sobbing, onto the floor.

"Someday you'll understand," Mother said angrily, her voice cracking and high-pitched. "Someday you'll be a mother, and then you'll know what it's like caring for a disobedient daughter. When she wants to run into traffic, or take some other insane risk, I hope that you'll be a good-enough mother and do whatever it takes to insure your daughter's safety. That's what I'm doing. Now get up; we're going home."

I cried all the way home, despite Mother's threats, and all the way up the elevator, and all the way into my room. I didn't have the tea set. I didn't have the jump rope; Mother had left its severed halves on the counter of Great Aunt Virginia's kitchen. I didn't have Great Aunt Virginia, and it looked like I was never again going to see her. For all that I knew, she might be trapped in

Arcadia forever. I was the new jumper and my jump rope was gone forever; *I'd failed everyone.*

At Mother's insistence, I changed my clothes, carefully hanging my dress in my closet; I wouldn't need it anymore, and it bore dozens of tiny cuts. Tears of frustration welled in my eyes, but I fought them back. I couldn't leave Great Aunt Virginia to Punch's foul mercy; Falcon had once been trapped in Princess Gracely's giant rhinestone, and Great Aunt Virginia had said that he couldn't have survived in it for long.

Ways to go back flitted through my mind; I could slip out the door while Mother was distracted, and run away, but what then? How was I, a penniless twelve year old girl, going to get to Baltimore when my magic jump rope was now severed in two? I considered busses, taxis, even stealing Mother's keys and driving myself, although I'd never driven anything but a virtual car, but I quickly rejected each idea. I wouldn't get far, and if the police caught me, then I'd get thrown into Juvenile Hall, from which I'd certainly never escape. Besides, Great Aunt Virginia would never approve.

A moment later, I opened my laptop and logged online. I couldn't do this alone; I needed help.

Audrey> HELP

Hilary> What?

Audrey> Virginia captured. Dolls captured. Mom cut the jump rope.

Hilary> NO!!!

Audrey> Yes. Need you ASAP!

Hilary> I'll sneak out.

Audrey> No, ask your mom.

Hilary> Why?

Audrey> I need you to bring clothes and make-up.

Hilary> Why?

Audrey> We have a new enemy. We need to look like them.

Hilary> On my way.

I closed my laptop and stood up. I had to take several deep breaths to steel my nerves, and then I marched out of my bedroom. Mother was wiping down the kitchen counters; I faced her resolutely.

"I have to go back."

Mother shook her head without even looking at me.

"You want to be a good mother. You want to protect me. Do you want me to learn to give up on friends and family whenever their needs become unpleasant?"

"This isn't unpleasant, it's dangerous," Mother said.

"Great Aunt Virginia would've risked anything to save you," I said.

"You will not talk to me that way!" Mother shouted angrily. "I'm your mother! You will not talk to me like an ... like an ..."

"... Like an adult?" I finished.

"You're not an adult; you're only twelve."

"Yes, but the lessons I'm learning today, right now, will stay with me forever. Friendship, loyalty, family, love ... and how to turn my back on those who love me."

"Aunt Virginia knew what she was getting herself into," Mother said. "She's an adult and can take whatever chances she wants."

"You're an adult, Mother. You can take a chance."

"Not with my daughter's life; I can't lose you."

"Like you lost Father?"

"How dare you!"

"Don't you see?" I pleaded. "Great Aunt Virginia knew the risks, and took them, for love, out of devotion to those who love her. That's what I want to do: be the kind of daughter that you want me to be. If I don't, if I don't at least try, then the only lesson I'll learn is to never love, to never trust anyone, ever again. Even a jump rope can't bridge that chasm; if you let Great Aunt Virginia die, then you'll lose me ... and yourself ... eventually ... and forever."

Mother closed her eyes, and I could almost feel the shudder that swept through her. I clenched my teeth to keep from speaking; I had nothing else to say. If this failed, if I failed, then my last hope would be gone.

The loud doorbell startled both of us. I

opened it, and Hilary stepped in, her arms full of designer shopping bags.

"What's this?" Mother demanded.

"Really, Mother, you didn't think that I'd try to rescue Great Aunt Virginia alone?"

A minute later, Hilary and I were alone in my room. I told her everything, mostly with tears leaking from my eyes. I described creepy Mr. Magee in The Palace, with its thick cobwebs and sunken roof, the castle-like Factory, about our losing the battle against the flying glamour dolls, how we found the baby dolls making glamour clothes in Punch's personal sweat-shop, and finally how Great Aunt Virginia, Hiram, Muskay, and Princess Gracely were trapped in the giant rhinestone, and how I was almost killed by the shadow puppets. When I explained how Mother cut the jump rope, I broke down, unable to continue.

"Glamour dolls!" Hilary exclaimed. "What kind of threat are glamour dolls?"

"You didn't see them," I said. "Thousands, enough to bury us in a mountain of plastic limbs and fake hair; Mr. Magee said that nothing could stop them."

"How are we going to stop them?" Hilary asked.

"We can't," I said. "Punch is the key; we need to stop Punch."

"How are we going to do that?"

"Not without powerful help," I said. "We need to rescue Judy."

"What's with the clothes and make-up?" Hilary asked.

"The glamour dolls are our biggest threat," I said. "We can't fight them, but they don't seem really evil; they wouldn't sacrifice one of their own to stop us. They worship fashions and appearances, so we need to look like them, at least long enough to rescue Judy."

"Will Judy help us?"

"Punch is her husband, and he locked her in a dark dungeon with her own paddle ...," I began. "She'll ..."

"She'll kill him," Hilary finished.

Hilary pulled out the contents of her designer bags. First came the make-up, of which she'd brought more than Mother owned, and this was only part of her collection. Then she pulled out several fancy outfits and a pile of jewelry, mostly plastic, and finally she withdrew an old, worn jump rope.

"First in, last out," Hilary said. "Do you think it'll work?"

"It has to ... or we're powerless," I said.

"Let's try it," Hilary said.

"Alright, but softly; don't let Mother hear."

Even taking it easy, I was instantly reminded that Hilary was better at jump roping than I. She jumped very lightly, but still did many tricks, like Jogging Steps, Leg-Over-Cross, and Speed Jumps;

she could flip the rope two, sometimes three times, under her for each jump. But no magic sparkled.

"You're trying too hard," I said, and when she stopped, I took the jump rope. "The magic's in the play, not in how hard you jump. You've played with dolls; you have to play with magic the same way."

I began jumping, and since Hilary had reminded me, I added in a few other tricks that we used to do; Skier, Double-Under, and Cross-Cross. The sparkles started almost at once, and then I quit; I didn't need to do magic now and couldn't afford to get exhausted.

"Let me try!" Hilary said excitedly.

"Remember, the magic is in the play," I warned. "When you get too serious, it's over."

Hilary started again. She went slower this time, calmer, and eventually gold and silver sparkles began to lightly shine. As her jump rope started to glow, Hilary caught her toe on the cord and tripped, staring amazed at the shimmering lights.

"Did you see that?" Hilary beamed, positively gleeful as she recovered her balance.

"Very good, but you have to get better fast," I said. "Not here; we'll practice in Arcadia, and you have to get used to the exhaustion; magic drains you very fast."

"I can't believe that it worked!" Hilary giggled. "We're going to be rich ... famous!"

"If we can't stop Punch then we're going to be dead," I reminded her. "Let's get ready. Which outfit is mine?"

The doorbell rang and we heard Mother's footsteps in the livingroom.

"Charlotte, what is it?"

"Hello, Madge; please come in."

The voice of Hilary's mother startled both of us, but their voices lowered instantly. Hilary and I crept to my door and pressed our ears against the wood, but we heard, only soft whispers and hushed exclamations. We stared at each other; this couldn't be good. They spoke for a good five minutes, but we never caught a word.

"Audrey!" Mother's voice called.

"Hilary!" her mother called.

Swallowing thick lumps in our throat, we trooped out. Both of our mothers stared at us; our faces were almost unrecognizable under the amount of gaudy make-up that we were wearing. I stared guiltily from under bright green eye shadow with silver glitter, and Hilary stared out from under violet eyelids with glittering gold specs. Our faces shined from moisturizer and foundation, and our hair was stiff with hairspray, making it look totally artificial. My lips were persimmon, and Hilary's lips were argent grape. Our clothes were equally outrageous; I wore all black with a short skirt, shorter than anything I owned, and I was laden with shining jewelry matching the glitter over my eyes. Hilary wore scarlet with fake rubies dangling from her ears, neck, wrists, and studded onto her metallic-gold-colored belt. I struggled to balance in high heels; Hilary had worn them before, but I was a novice to stilettos, even if they were child-sized.

Never had I seen such disapproving glares.

"Do you know what you two look like?" Hilary's mother asked.

"Glamour dolls?" I said hesitantly.

Both women exchanged glances.

"Are you ready?" Mother asked us.

"For what?" Hilary asked, undisguised fear raising her voice to a squeak.

"Ready to go to Baltimore," Mother said. "Madge wants to see."

"I'm driving," Hilary's mother said.

Only Hilary's face looked more surprised than mine.

"You're not ready," Mother said sternly. "Aren't you forgetting something?"

We exchanged a glance.

"My jump rope!" Hilary exclaimed, and she ran back to my bedroom to get it.

Nervously I stared around our living room, self-conscious under two mother's stares. I couldn't go to Arcadia empty-handed. On impulse, I grabbed two of my beloved stuffed animals, my Pegasus and my purple dragon. Both mothers grabbed their purses, and we headed out the door.

No one spoke during the whole drive to Baltimore.

Mother and Hilary's mother kept looking at each other with secretive smiles on their faces. In the back seat, we sat in belted silence. Hilary had her jump rope in her hands and I clutched my stuffed animals; I'd forgotten how soft they were and how I used to spend endless hours playing with them, flying them all around my room, not able to sleep without them beside my pillow to protect me during the long, dark night. I'd loved them, and deep inside, I suspected that I still did. Now I held them tightly again, protectively; never had I needed them so desperately.

We reached Great Aunt Virginia's apartment building and parked right in front. Six boys were lazing on her steps, and when Hilary and I got out of the car, the slothful boys broke out laughing. I felt humiliated, wearing this revoltingly-flashy costume and painted like a woman of unfavorable reputation. As we approached the steps, all six boys rose to confront us.

"Get out of our way," Mother said forcefully.

The boys said nothing, just stared insolently at us.

"Step aside!" Mother shouted.

"You got a problem?" one of the boys asked.

"These girls got no problem," another boy said, and several of the boys laughed. "Leave them with us!"

"Step back," Hilary's mother said to us, and we

obeyed as she reached into her purse. "I don't have a problem: I have a gun."

To my amazement, Hilary's mother lifted a real pistol, just like the ones on TV, and pointed it at the boys. They froze, some trying to seem tough, but most looked just plain scared.

"Charlotte, did you hear these boys just threaten our daughters?"

"I sure did, Madge."

"Good: then this is perfectly legal," Hilary's mother said.

"No jury is going to believe a bunch of dead hoodlums over two respectable housewives," Mother added.

Suddenly one of the boys held up his empty hands, and a moment later, he was running down the street as fast as he could. The other boys just stared at Hilary's mother's cold steel barrel pointing at them, and then they slowly walked down the steps and slunk after their cowardly friend. They walked calmly backwards for their first few steps down the sidewalk, and then they turned and shuffled quickly away.

We hurried up the stairs and Mother unlocked Great Aunt Virginia's door with the key that she'd taken to lock Great Aunt Virginia's door behind us. We rushed inside and locked the main entrance behind us. Soon we entered Great Aunt Virginia's exotic apartment, which was familiar to Mother and I. Hilary and her mother stared, amazed and agape, their eyes roaming hungrily all over the apartment.

"Look at all these antiques!" Hilary's mother said as she examined the beautiful lamps and countless dolls. "In perfect condition; do you know what these are worth?"

"There are books over there," Mother said, for she knew that Hilary's mom collected rare volumes.

"This is it, isn't it?" Hilary asked, staring at the tiny table. "This is Hiram, Muskay, and Princess Gracely?"

Hilary knelt to examine the dolls and tea set while her mom went for the books. I headed for the kitchen.

"I'll make the tea," I said.

"I'll boil the water," Mother said.

I selected as best I could; some of Great Aunt Virginia's tan clay herb jars were getting low. I picked the few that I knew best and carefully smelled the rest, then dumped all that I'd selected into the pestle and ground them finely with the mortar. By the time that Mother had the water hot, I was ready. I spooned in the powder and Mother set the teapot aside to steep.

"Can I pick this up?" Hilary's mom asked Mother, pointing at one of the oldest volumes. "I can't believe I'm looking at a first edition; I've been to rare book exhibitions and never seen one."

Mother allowed it, knowing that Great Aunt Virginia would insist, and that Hilary's mother knew everything there was to know about handling antique books. Hilary was roaming about the room, careful not to touch anything, staring into every nook and corner.

"The tea's ready," Mother finally said, and she reached into her purse and lifted out of it the spare jump rope that she'd purchased, and she gave it to me. I thanked her with glowing, grateful eyes, and tied the jump rope around my waist. Hilary watched me intently and did the same with hers.

"Audrey, Hilary, I know that you can return if you want to," Mother said. "I want you both to promise me that, if you get into any danger at all, you'll come back right away; you won't wait for anything ... not even Great Aunt Virginia."

Hilary's mom stared at us from beside the bookshelf, trying to understand. Silently I wondered what Mother had told her.

"I promise," I said to Mother, and Hilary repeated my oath.

Hilary's mom carefully returned the faded red volume of David Copperfield and then sat on the couch by Mother. I took Muskay from his chair and let Mother hold him in her lap, then made Hilary sit across from me at the table. Hilary gave me a disgusted look as I directed her to sit in the little girl's chair, but I glared her into silent compliance. I brought my Pegasus and purple dragon to the table and sat them before me on opposite sides of my plate, both facing me so that I could watch their faces. Would they move as the dizziness overtook us? I wanted to believe in them so much!

When everyone was seated, each with an empty cup before them, I poured. I started with Hilary's mom and complemented everyone. Hilary's mom looked startled when I told her that I always admired her beautiful hair, and when I told Muskay that he was looking delightfully mischievous today, Hilary's jaw fell and she stared at me as if I were mad. But I continued, and when I got to Hilary, I told her how beautiful she looked and that I was sure that her belief in the magic would propel her to places beyond her imagination. Lastly, I poured my own tea, sat in Muskay's chair and smiled. I had my two favorite dolls beside me, a jump rope, and hot tea in the magic tea set: *I was going back to Arcadia.*

"The magic's in the play," I reminded Hilary, and then Mother and I reached for our teacups, and Hilary and her mother followed our example.

The tea wasn't as sweet as I preferred, but it was warm and flavorful, rich in its own way, almost too strong. I blew away the steam and sipped it. Soon we were all drinking, Hilary excited, her mother watchful, and Mother slightly nervous; I was the only one ready to go.

The accustomed dizziness took a bit longer, but it finally came. As the tingle overwhelmed me, the golden wings on my Pegasus fluttered and a tiny red flame slipped from the mouth of my purple dragon. I smiled, and then Great Aunt Virginia's apartment completely faded away.

Chapter 13

Into The Fire

A bright blue sky, dotted with tiny cream-puff clouds, opened over us. Hilary looked up, startled, as if truly believing in Arcadia for the first time. I glanced around; we were in a yellow-flowered field surrounded by forest; the very field where I'd first appeared in Arcadia, near where I'd freed Falcon from the first giant rhinestone.

"Stop staring; we've work to do," I said to Hilary, and I took off my jump rope and held it ready. Hilary seemed too amazed to hear me, but her hands fumbled her rope off her waist and slowly held it open.

"Hilary!" I shouted. "Stop daydreaming; people's lives depend on us!"

"Yea, ours," Hilary said.

I frowned and started jump roping.

"Magic light,
Shine bright,

Wake my friend
From her fright."

Almost instantly my jump rope began to sparkle, but Hilary ignored my barb and recited the chant with me, jumping her rope with ease. We just Double Jumped as the tall grass interfered with our swings, and occasionally the bud of a yellow flower would fly up into the air, severed by our skipping cords. Sparkles began on Hilary's jump rope very slowly, and her eyes widened with amazement as her jump rope's sparkles grew brighter. My hope was that Hilary, having already known about the magic, would be less susceptible to its drain. Still, I broke my chant to urge encouragement.

"Concentrate," I said. "Focus on the play; that's the magic."

Soon our jump ropes shined brightly, and then I stopped us both.

"Good; light is our only weapon against the shadow puppets," I said. "Now we're going to try something harder. A shield charm; you'll need that, too."

Hilary took some time to get the shield charm to work. I trained her exactly as Great Aunt Virginia had trained me, and before Hilary expanded her golden sphere beyond the range of her jump rope, sweat was dripping down her face and she was breathing in gasps.

"That should do it," I said.

"That's ... it?" Hilary gasped. "I ... want to know ... everything."

"Not now," I said. "I can't let you get exhausted; to

save Great Aunt Virginia we must both be rested and ready."

"What ... am I ... going to do?" Hilary asked.

"Protect yourself ... at all costs," I said. "The last thing that I'm going to teach you doesn't require a jump rope; you need to know how to fade back to our world."

"Go back ...?" Hilary asked.

"In case we fail," I said. "If you get into trouble, fade back and escape."

"How?"

"When the fear overwhelms you, call for your mother," I said. "That's what worked for me."

"I don't want to go back."

"You will. I'm going to be the decoy; once we get into The Factory, I'm going to fight Punch, but I can't beat him."

"Then ... why ...?"

"While I'm fighting Punch, you're going to slip down the stairs, using the light-spell to drive back the shadow puppets, and free Judy."

Hilary looked worried.

"Do you think that I can?"

"Shadow puppets have no real substance; they're made of darkness and fear," I said. "If you can keep your rope glowing, you can skip across the room and lift the big paddle off her door. If you can't, if the shadow puppets get you, then fade back right away. Hilary, this land isn't safe; we could die here, and we will, if we don't fade back when we must. Promise me that you'll return before you get killed!"

"I promise."

"Good," I said. "Now, come stand beside me; I'm going to take us somewhere."

"Where?" Hilary asked.

"To the only friend that we have left."

"Can't we jump together?"

Gladly I tied my jump rope tight around my waist and Hilary and I stood shoulder-to-shoulder. I took one end of her jump rope and she held the other, and as we hadn't done for years, we started to jump together.

"Falcon! Falcon!
Wherever you hide!
Falcon! Falcon!
To your side!"

Hilary quickly picked up this simple chant, and faster, and with less energy than I'd thought possible, suddenly the clearing around us faded with each pass of the jump rope, and a familiar hill faded in. The last thing I saw was a huge pair of birds flying in the distance ... and then they were gone.

We appeared jumping together right on top of a wide grassy hill by a stream. Right next to our feet were several small holes pouring smoke out of the ground. All around us were bright flowers, but no flowers shone brighter than the hundred neon tufts of dazzlingly-colored hair sticking up from the little figures gathered on the long, tiny marble steps.

"What ...! Where ...?" Hilary asked, but I strode on ahead.

"This is Troll Hill, just like I told you," I said. "Come on; this is ridiculous."

We were standing on the highest crest; Hilary followed me down the side of Troll Hill. Smiling troll faces lifted and beamed at us as we approached. Many little trolls were all standing outside of the two magnificent marble doors, which were flanked by large, white-framed windows built into the very side of the hill. The marble doors were closed.

Hilary stared at the short, stubby trolls, only five inches tall, with their wide ears and toothy grins, bright, energetic eyes, and fluffy neon-colored tufts of hair which rose straight up over their heads. I stepped up to the marble doors, seized the brass rings on them, and pulled. The stone doors swung open easily, and inside the main troll hall, sitting down and hunched over, filling most of their hall, sat Falcon.

"Audrey!" Falcon smiled. "So glad to see you!"

"Hiding while yours friends are in danger: you should be ashamed!"

"Cowards live longer than heroes ..."

"Get out of there!"

At my disapproving glare, Falcon scooted and wedged himself out of the cramped troll hall. Many other trolls were in the hall, squeezed into the corners, and they followed him outside. Falcon extricated himself and stood, stretching his joints in the sunlight.

"Something terrible happened, didn't it?" Falcon asked.

"Punch is back," I said. "He's got an army of glamour dolls and shadow puppets. He's taken over The Factory, has the baby dolls slaving for him, and he's captured Princess Gracely, Hiram, Muskay, and Great Aunt Virginia."

Falcon considered this, and then started to climb back inside the troll's main hall.

"No, you don't!" I said, grabbing his arm.

"What do you want me to do, fight Punch?" Falcon argued. "This is the time to hide!"

"We're all going to fight Punch," I said. "The trolls, the hand puppets, the marionettes, the rag dolls; all of us, and that includes you."

"What can I do?" Falcon whined.

"You can help us gather the dolls," I said. "Come, we need to get everyone; we're raising all of Arcadia to fight for its freedom."

"Trolls and rag dolls against Punch and shadow puppets?" Falcon asked.

"This is Hilary: a second jumper," I said to Falcon, and he looked at her, amazed. "With two jumpers, we're going to attack The Factory and rescue our friends."

"What do you need me for?" Falcon asked.

"To stand right beside me," I said, and I forcibly

took his hand. "Where's Mr. Stoney?"

"Me Stoney," Stoney came forward, out of the marble doors.

I smiled at him. Stoney was a little taller and much heavier, and his hair was even thicker than the others, far less kempt, and shocking pink. Upon his right cheek was his ugly, jagged scar, but he was the smartest troll, and therefore their leader.

"Mr. Stoney," I curtsied to him. "We've found the source of all badness in Arcadia, but we need help driving it out."

"Trolls always help!" Stoney said in his deep voice.

"We need all trolls to go straight from here to The Factory; can you do that?"

"Trolls go to Factory!" Stoney shouted, and all the trolls cheered.

As one, the trolls turned and ran downhill toward their creek. More trolls than I had imagined lived here; suddenly they began pouring out of their main hall and every other door and hole in Troll Hill. All of them cheered and ran to follow the others.

"Stupid trolls," Falcon sneered.

"Falcon, which way is The Factory from here?"

Falcon startled at the question, and then he smiled and pointed toward the forest.

"Don't make me use the jump rope on you," I warned.

Falcon frowned, turned his finger, and pointed across the fields. I shouted to the trolls, showed them the new direction, and after only a moment of confusion, they turned and excitedly ran as I directed, eager to help.

"They'll never make it, and even if they do, trolls are useless," Falcon said.

"They'll get their chance to prove their worth," I said. "Come; we've many places to visit."

Our next stop was at the fort of the tin soldiers. Hilary and I brought Falcon with us, and Hilary stared wide-eyed as I shouted for General Walnut.

"It's like a whole world of doll houses!" Hilary exclaimed.

"You'll get used to it," I smiled.

On an outside balcony of their main hall, over the front doors, General Walnut appeared with his seven other garishly-uniformed nutcracker dolls, all with comically bushy beards, mustaches, and eyebrows of fake fur.

"Another jumper?" General Walnut's wide mouth flapped on its hinge. "Improper! Disgraceful! Unauthorized!"

"Please, General Walnut," I said. "Great Aunt Virginia, Hiram, Muskay, and Princess Gracely have been captured. You've got to help us."

"Impossible," General Walnut said, and all the other nutcrackers bobbed their solid-wooden heads in agreement with him. "We're received no formal reports. Unprecedented. Improper protocol."

"Punch is leading them," I argued. "He's come back."

"Punch?" General Walnut asked. "Punch was banished. Champion military exercise; we have forms and documents to prove it, notarized by the paper dolls. Punch back? Tish-tosh!"

"We found the baby dolls," I said. "They're at The Factory ... being forced to make clothes and make-up for Punch's glamour dolls."

"Baby dolls?" General Walnut asked. "The missing babies?"

"Yes," I said forcefully. "As the chief jumper for all of Arcadia, I am making a formal report; the baby dolls are at The Factory."

"Highly irregular!" General Walnut said.

"You have standing orders, don't you, to find and rescue the baby dolls?" Falcon asked. "Don't you have a whole division on stand-by, awaiting report of where the baby dolls are? Three squads of tin soldiers have vanished; don't you want to rescue them, too?"

General Walnut looked very disturbed, then conferred momentarily with his advisors, the other nutcracker dolls, all of whom whispered incoherently as they clumsily knocked their wooden heads together, all talking, and none listening. Finally, General Walnut turned and faced us.

"So be it!" General Walnut shouted. "To battle! Summon all units, every tin soldier! Ready cannon and powder! Prepare the march! Forward, to The Factory ... and victory!"

Three of the nutcracker generals pulled out little brass horns and lifted them to their painted lips. The tiny trumpets sounded, and hundreds of tin soldiers turned and marched toward the hall.

Worried, Hilary turned to me.

"These ... are what's going to help us?" she asked.

"The magic's in the play," I reminded her. "The game ... is to win ... but it's still a game."

More tin soldiers rushed out of the many smaller buildings, and even more came marching double-time over the hills. Shortly afterwards, with General Walnut and his other nutcracker dolls in the lead, an army of over a thousand tin soldiers formed into long, straight lines, and marched off toward The Factory, in step with dozens of drummers rat-a-tat-tatting, while military flags and banners streamed over their heads.

"Whose next, the farthest from The Factory?" I asked Falcon.

"The paper dolls," Falcon said.

"They can't help," I said. "The paper dolls couldn't endure the wind of buzzing wings. Do we go to the marionettes, the hand puppets, or the rag dolls?"

Reluctantly, Falcon relented. Minutes later, the walled fort of the tin soldiers faded as our jump rope passed over our eyes, and the wagon-mounted wooden stages of the marionettes appeared. However, just as we faded, I caught a glimpse of the same two great winged creatures flying high in the sky, but we faded away before I could make them out.

"Isn't this too fast?" Falcon asked worriedly after we'd transported to Theater City. "Shouldn't we wait, maybe come up with a plan?"

"We can't wait," I said. "You wouldn't have survived inside the rhinestone if I'd waited, and at sunset, the shadow puppets can emerge. We've got to strike while we can."

Loud stomps of many wooden boots repeatedly crashed in unison, making a rhythm of sudden clatters. The largest cart-borne stage, from which all the noise was coming, had its thick velvet curtains closed, and Master Strand's commanding voice shouted, "No, no: it's kick, step, stomp-stomp, kick!"

As we reached the main stage, I pulled open the red velvet curtains, revealing three dozen marionettes dangling from their strings, standing in two groups of six rows, all with tiny muskets over their shoulders. They startled as they saw us, and Master Strand turned around to see what disturbed them.

"No, jumper, no!" Master Strand shouted, waving his hands to distract me. "This is rehearsal; we're not ready!"

"Rehearsal-time is over," I said. "We're at war. Punch is back; he kidnapped the baby dolls and made them into slaves. He has glamour dolls and shadow puppets backing him, but we have a plan. The trolls and tin soldiers are already enroute to Punch's Factory; we're going to take him down."

I quickly described how Great Aunt Virginia, Princess Gracely, Hiram and Muskay had been captured, but Master Strand cut me off before I finished.

"We know this dance, jumper," Master Strand said. "Marionettes, Arcadia is threatened; rehearsal is finished. The curtain rises, and by our strings, we must perform!"

The marionettes all cheered, then started pulling down their cross-braces and hitching them over their shoulders.

"We're rallying everyone," I told Master Strand. "We'll meet you there."

"We won't miss this queue," Master Strand promised.

Next, we jump-roped to the workshop of the hand puppets. I let Hilary do the jumping and steadied her as she quickly tired from its magical exertion. A great noise of hammering and sawing thundered as we arrived. We entered their workshop through the biggest doors, which even the stage-covered carts of the marionettes could drive through, and shouted through the flying sawdust for all construction to stop. The many workers, busy making a new doll house for the rag dolls, stopped their tools in mid-stroke and stared at us.

"What's this?" Boss Fist shouted, coming forward in

his metal construction hat. "Who ordered you to stop?"

"I did," I said, and I repeated my message to Boss Fist as I had to the trolls, the tin soldiers, and the marionettes. He listened intently, bowed deeply as I introduced Hilary as a new jumper, and finally promised to aid us.

"Arcadia can't go to war without us lending a hand!" Boss Fist shouted, and all of the puppets cheered.

While unimpressed with the other dolls, and doubtful of their effectiveness, Hilary's smile widened when she saw the cheering hand puppets lift hammers, saws, and razor-sharp wood-chisels as weapons. The hand puppets seemed more practical, as if they understood the coming battle more-clearly than their fellow dolls; their expressions were grim and their weapons deadly.

"We need to rally our town and bring all of our kind," Boss Fist said.

"We'll meet you at The Factory," I promised. "We have one last stop to make."

Hilary exclaimed delightedly as we reached the village of the rag dolls. The large Victorian dollhouses enchanted her, and she stooped and looked in the windows as much as she could, admiring the stylish antique furniture ... and frightening many peaceful rag dolls as her huge face filled their tiny windows. I hurried on to the stitchery, where I could hear the wide looms clacking as the rag dolls worked them.

"Mistress Flax!" I cried through the high windows. "Please, we need to talk!"

Work on the new fabrics stopped, and through the wide windows, all of the rag dolls stared nervously up at us as Falcon, Hilary, and I stood filling the street between their four-foot Victorian houses.

"Where's Virginia the Grand?" Mistress Flax demanded when she appeared on her balcony. "What's the meaning of this? Stop production ...? There better be an emergency ...!"

"Virginia the Grand has been captured," I said, "along with Princess Gracely, Muskay, and Hiram."

Mistress Flax stared without comment as I repeated my warning and our dire need. She nodded to Hilary when I introduced her, after briefly glancing at Falcon, who obviously didn't want to be there. Her expression never softened, and by the time that I'd finished, her angry, snarling face resembled a second grade teacher that I'd once had who couldn't speak to children without shouting, and she glared so furiously that I thought she'd bust her stitches. The pink dye on her cheeks turned crimson.

"We rag dolls shall mend all that we can," Mistress Flax promised, anger crisping her serious tone. Like the hand puppets, the rag dolls seemed to understand the unfortunate consequences of war. "We'll be there, with scissors, pinking shears, button hooks, and every weapon that we have. The Factory's not far from here; we won't be long."

"We'll see you there," I said. "We'll scout ahead and ..."

"You'll be very careful and take no chances!" Mistress Flax glared up at us. "Without jumpers, we don't have a prayer."

"Yes, Mistress Flax," I promised respectfully ... as if I wasn't talking to a doll less than ten inches tall.

Mistress Flax dismissed us as if she were our superior, and we carefully threaded our way out of their lovely village, and several rag dolls ran indoors to keep from getting trampled as we cautiously stepped around them.

Once we were outside the village, past the last house, Hilary met my eyes.

"That's it, right?" Hilary asked. "Now we're going to war?"

"Yes," I said. "Without us, the good dolls will be massacred."

"This is the part where we could die," Hilary frowned.

"Every person who ever became famous had to overcome some obstacle," I said. "This is ours; are you going to shy away now?"

My question seemed to fortify Hilary; Arcadia was still too new to entirely believe, even though she'd seen everything. But Hilary seemed to harden, to grow determined, as I looked at her.

"Nothing stops me from winning," Hilary promised.

We jump-roped to the top of a distant hill facing The Factory, not nearly as close as where the flying fairies had waylaid us.

"Now we wait," I said.

"For what?" Hilary asked.

"We can't afford to get caught," I said. "Punch is bad enough, but the countless glamour dolls would overwhelm us; we need for the others to start the battle, and once they're engaged, then we sneak into The Factory and face Punch."

"Why can't we just jump rope into the dungeon and free Judy?" Hilary asked.

"The dungeon's not small; we'd risk getting lost," I said. "Besides, the shadow puppets would be on us before we finished jumping, if we landed in their midst. Once we get into the main chamber, I'll nod to the stairs to Judy's prison cell. Once Punch and I are engaged, then you run down the stairs; use the spell for light to drive back the shadow puppets. Pull off the paddle that bars Judy's door, and that should be it. If you can't get back up to me, then fade back home and ..."

"I'm not fading home!" Hilary argued.

"When the fear of the shadow puppets smothers you, you'll change your mind," I said. "Don't lose your head; if fear and darkness cover you, call for your mother."

Hilary nodded, but she never said that she would. I let the matter drop.

"Look, here they come!" Falcon said.

In the distance, little figures appeared marching over the hills. Hundreds of trolls came first, with their neon-colored hair shining in the sunlight, and more trolls followed in a long line behind them. A thousand tin soldiers appeared not far away, marching in ordered lines, and then came the stringed marionettes, the hand puppets wielding their deadly wood-working tools, and finally the rag dolls, carrying sharp sewing instruments, all designed for cutting and piercing. The five armies surged forward, covering the hills.

Horns blew from The Factory. Winged glamour dolls, only glowing colored specs from our distant vantage, flew out of The Factory and winged up into the sky, surveying the approaching armies. Some flew down to get closer views, but then all swooped back inside The Factory. The horns continued to blow.

"We've rung the doorbell," Hilary said.

I nodded, frowning. I glanced at the sun, which was only an hour from setting; *we were cutting this close.*

Out of the castle marched the glamour doll army. Thousands and thousands poured out of the main gate, marching quickly on their abnormally long legs. Outfits of all colors and styles shined, twinkling from tiny gems, sequins, and tons of glitter reflecting the bright sunlight. By comparison, the five attacking armies looked drab and tiny; the glamour dolls outnumbered all of their opponents combined, many carried scalpels, and they marched in ordered formations that only the tin soldiers could match.

Closer and closer the two fronts approached, each relentless, determined to win, one side to preserve Arcadia as it had always been, the other to wash away the old ways and install a new order, ruled by Punch, for the sole benefit of him and his evil allies. Neither side slowed; the five armies marched over the last hill without stopping, and the countless glamour dolls crossed the clearing and marched up the hill, ready to meet their foes.

The battle met in a flurry of vicious combat. Dolls normally innocent and non-threatening engaged in violence only seen on the toughest battlefields. Trolls charged into the fray, heedless of slices striking and scratching their tough hides, and any glamour doll that their hands seized became a club used against other glamour dolls. The sharp scalpels couldn't cut deep through the wood of the nutcrackers, or the metal skins of the tin soldiers, and the *cracks!* of their musket-fire blew back the glittery glamour dolls. Many marionettes were casting their cross-braces over the closest glamour dolls, entangling the stiff-armed dolls in their strings.

The hand puppets attacked with most-deadly results, smashing glamour dolls flat with hammers, sending plastic arms and legs flying over the battle, and driving chisels deep through their foes' exotic, colorful fashions. But the hand puppets were mostly cloth, and the scalpels of the glamour dolls slashed deep rents through them. The rag dolls suffered even worse, stuffing bursting from their soft bodies, but as we watched, Mistress Flax rose above her followers, with a curved edging tool, and slashed off the pony-tail of the glamour doll that she was fighting, who reached up with one hand and felt her ruined, severed tresses, and then screamed in horror and ran away.

All of the five armies charged into battle, but the gates of The Factory were still spewing legions of glamour dolls in seemingly endless numbers.

"Time to go," I said, and Hilary nodded.

"No, wait!" Falcon said. "Look what's coming!"

Falcon was staring up into the sky. Far above us flew the two giant winged figures I'd seen flying towards us twice before.

"What is it?" Hilary cried as they approached, their wingspan seeming wider with each flap.

"I don't know!" I cried. "I've never seen ...!"

But I had seen them, and not just glimpsed them from great distances. My eyes widened in disbelief for the first time in ages; not since I'd first come to Arcadia had I been this surprised.

The two great figures flew down from the sky, buffeting us with terrible gusts as they flapped their powerful wings. They landed before us; one was a tall horse, strong and gleaming white, with large gold wings. The other was taller, thicker, and far more menacing, with rough, dark-violet scales and long fangs, burning red eyes, and a glow coming from its mouth of deep fires smoldering inside it. Laughter burst from me while Hilary stood shaking; while I loved them in my world, in Arcadia, my Pegasus and purple dragon were real.

"Allow me," Falcon said to Hilary, who looked as if she wanted to fade and never see another doll again. Falcon lifted Hilary and set her on the back of my Pegasus, and my purple dragon bowed low to let me clamber onto his back. I mounted the dragon without fear; these were my dolls: my love made them real.

We rode to The Factory like avenging angels over the heads of the combatants, all of whom screamed in outrage or terror or delight. The glamour dolls before the gates of The Factory scattered before us, and we dismounted and drew our jump ropes as other heroes might draw mighty swords. The glamour dolls drew back from us, but they leapt upon the legs of the purple dragon, easily clinging to his rough scales, and my Pegasus neighed in pain as scalpels stabbed at his ankles.

"Fly off!" I shouted at them. "We can take it from here!"

"Help our friends!" Hilary shouted as their mighty wings beat the air and blasted up a cloud of dust, but I was already jump roping, singing loud.

"Drive back!

Drive back!
Drive a-way!
Out of
Our path
You must stay!"

The glamour dolls blocking the entrance to The Factory flew backwards as my spell struck. Through the open path, I ran inside, my jump rope blasting before me as I went. Hilary ran in behind me, and together we charged across the long hall of frightened baby dolls, who had crowded together against the walls, abandoning their tiny sewing machines as the clamor of battle raged outside, and many had started to cry real tears.

Flying glamour dolls zipped toward us, scalpels raised.

"Separate!" I shouted to Hilary, and she dashed to one side while I went to the other.

My flashing cord blasted them back, but they came on again. The closer that they came, the farther back I blasted them, but each returned almost instantly. I chanted and jumped harder, but to no avail; the flying fairies kept coming, one after another.

"Enough of this!" Hilary shouted, and she began Speed-Jumping, her rope flashing as fast as she could flip it, passing several times under her with each jump as she leapt closer, step by step. I matched her Speed-Jumping, and Hilary's magic, added to mine, blasted the winged fairies upwards until they smacked against the high ceiling, unable to be pushed back any farther; the winged fairies had enough after that. With scowls and glares of fury, they pushed off of the ceiling and flittered out through high, thin windows, escaping from us entirely.

The frightened baby dolls stared at us, some still crying, but I didn't have time to console them; I nodded toward the large doorway at the end of the hall, and we ran through it.

There stood Punch, before all of the empty shelves of the glamour doll beds and the giant TV, which was now displaying a commercial for designer shoes which *'no woman could live without'*. Punch was hammering his giant paddle against the magic rhinestone, which was now covered with so many cracks that Great Aunt Virginia, Princess Gracely, Hiram, and Muskay were mere shadows within the fractured crystal.

"Jumper!" Punch cried, turning to me. "Now I don't have to hunt you down!"

"You'll be hunting for your head when I'm done!" I shouted, and I whirled my jump rope in one hand and slashed at Punch.

Punch turned his paddle against it, and the two clanged resoundingly with a magical blast. Punch cursed, counter-attacked, and I met his paddle forcefully, but as our second blow knocked me backward, I glanced at Hilary and pointed to the tiny alcove through which the candlelit stairs descended. Hilary nodded, then dashed off.

"Who was that?" Punch demanded, seeing Hilary.

"No one that you'll live long enough to know!" I shouted, and I attacked again.

Punch and I fought alone. The Factory rung with the fierceness of our blows, blasted by sudden winds whipping about us each time that our blades met. I struggled, and forced myself to keep fighting, when I noticed that the giant rhinestone was clearing, its countless cracks resealing, becoming restored. I pressed my assault, but the magical blasts of our clashes drove us apart each time that we re-engaged. I needed to keep Punch busy; if I could distract him long enough for Hilary ...

Hilary's terrified scream pierced The Factory, resounding off every stone. I hesitated, and Punch smiled widely.

"Shadow puppets take no prisoners," Punch leered. "Your foolish companion has perished ... and now it's your turn!"

I stepped back; *Hilary? Dead?* No, she couldn't ... her mother would never forgive me. Punch advanced, but I stood frozen, unable to raise my jump rope. Punch grinned wickedly and raised his powerful paddle.

Stones shattered, and a great hole burst open in the floor. A massive head rose out of the rubble, terrible, furious, a face like Punch's, but her head covered with a red scarf, concealing long, thick yellow hair, and wearing painted blue eye-shadow upon her lids.

"Punch!" Judy screamed, and her voice bellowed louder than any siren. "Husband! How dare you?"

Punch gasped, frozen in disbelief, and stared at his wife. Judy rose up into the hall, a giant puppet, a marionette without strings, a giant paddle matching Punch's weapon tight in her knotted fist. She was huge, and anger reddened every inch of her skin, almost matching the scarlet of her dress.

"Stay back, wife!" Punch growled. "Arcadia is mine!"

"Never!" Judy shouted, and she raised her massive paddle.

Punch and Judy struck at each other viscously, their paddles clanging deafeningly, far louder than my jump rope, and the blasts from their blows drove me back against the alcove door. Hilary came running up the stairs, and relief washed over me.

"You're alive!" I shouted joyously.

"Just barely," Hilary grinned back at me. "When Judy came out of her prison, her expression was so murderous that I screamed at the sight of it."

"Come on!" I shouted over the clamor of Punch and Judy's fighting.

Through the gale-force winds tearing at our ridiculous fashions, Hilary and I forced our way across the hall. Punch and Judy slashed and hammered at each other, barely aware of us. We threw ourselves against the fractured rhinestone, clutching at it despite the sharp edges of its cracks.

"Princess Gracely!" I shouted. "Now! Lower the crystal!"

As I'd seen before, when Falcon was saved, the rhinestone began to shrink, to melt before my eyes. As it reduced and faded, Muskay was released first, but he only collapsed onto the others as they revived, and then they all fell to the stone floor. They looked exhausted, and gasped air as if their lungs had never breathed before.

"Great Aunt Virginia!" I cried over the blasting winds, and I grabbed Muskay, who laid on top, and helped pull him up, then struggled to assist Great Aunt Virginia to her feet. Hilary helped Princess Gracely to stand, and Muskay weakly helped pull Hiram to his thick, shaky boots.

Great Aunt Virginia stood unbalanced, and I struggled to steady her.

"No!" Great Aunt Virginia wheezed. "You must ... help Judy!"

I nodded, and glanced at Hilary to make sure that she'd heard. Hilary nodded back to me, and together we stood, leaning into the blustering winds, our jump ropes ready.

"Punch is bad!
Punch is tall!
Punch is weak!
Punch must fall!"

I shouted it into the wind, and Hilary recited with me on my second chant. As one, we began to jump, our chant never ceasing, our jump ropes slapping in perfect unison with our voices. Our magic cords began to sparkle at once, and their shimmering glows surrounded us. Finally, beams burst from our magical spheres, blasting across the hall, striking Punch, and driving him backwards against the screen of the giant T.V, which was now portraying seven smiling models in bikinis. Punch screamed as he was knocked aside, and Judy swung her paddle, swishing it through the gusty air, and struck the side of Punch's head.

"No!" Punch cried as he fell back, dazed but not defeated. "Not when I've come so far! My warriors! Come! Rescue your king! Make-up! Fashions! Beauty extraordinaire!"

"No!" Judy cried, and she lifted her paddle and struck again. But Punch, though pinned to the wall by our twin magical beams, raised his paddle to deflect hers just at the last second, and the clang of their weapons resounded across Arcadia.

Hilary and I kept jumping, focusing, and chanting, pouring our beams of magic at Punch. Great Aunt Virginia, Princess Gracely, Muskay, and Hiram shouted encouragement, but I was starting to feel the strain of too much magic. Hilary looked fully determined, but sweat glistened upon her brow. Still, we kept up our attack, refusing to relent.

"Glamour dolls!" Muskay cried, and Princess

Gracely screamed.

Behind us, crossing the hall of baby dolls, came the army of glamour dolls, marching swiftly on their elongated legs. Many had mussed hair, torn clothes, and sequins hanging by ragged threads, but they came on, their expressions furious. Above them, coming slow but determined, came the flying fairies, their wings beating the air.

"We can't let them reach us!" Hilary cried.

"We can't stop holding Punch!" I shouted.

"You take Punch!" Hilary shouted.

In mid-jump, Hilary turned around and began an X-to-Straddle, and then a Toe Exchange. Her beam striking Punch faded, but a strong breeze blew back the fake hair from the thousand plastic heads faced toward us. As she continued her fancy jumps, her breeze grew stronger. She did an Irish Fling, a Wounded Duck, and a Front Back Cross. The advancing glamour dolls were halted, straining against Hilary's strong winds, and the flying fairies were blown backwards, though still fighting to advance.

I matched Hilary, doing moves that I hadn't tried for years. I did a Behind the Back Cross, a Double Under, and a Leg-Over Cross. I loved doing fancy jumps, and my beam pinning Punch strengthened; Punch cried out, barely deflecting Judy's relentless attacks, and Great Aunt Virginia cheered.

But we gained no advantage. Hilary and I did Push-ups, Rump Jumps, and Between Knee Crosses, and the strength of our magic grew, but our exhaustion mounted, and the strain only increased. Punch began to fight back, pushing against the beam that I was pinning him with. Great Aunt Virginia was watching us intently, amazed by our acrobatics, but worry lined her face.

"Audrey!" Hilary gasped, and I looked back to see her barely managing to keep jumping. Sweat rained off her; she wasn't used to this strain, and I couldn't keep it up much longer. I kept up my chant, but Hilary had stopped chanting, gasping for each breath, and the army of glamour dolls advanced in the face of her weakening magic.

Finally Hilary faltered; Hiram rushed forward and caught her, or Hilary would've crashed to the floor. She fainted, closing her eyes. All of the flying fairies dashed forward, and before I could turn or change my chant, the flying fairies fouled my jump rope and my magic failed.

"Yes!" Punch cheered, and he drove Judy back with a vicious blow, and then jumped to his feet, away from the giant TV screen, and he rose, taller and more-menacing than ever.

Muskay grabbed Great Aunt Virginia and Princess Gracely and pulled them back, away from the advancing glamour dolls. Hiram retreated with them, Hilary unconscious in his arms. The flying glamour dolls glared at me with wicked triumph in their eyes; I couldn't fight them alone.

"No!" I shouted, and I swung my jump rope at them, making them scatter. Then, as they reoriented, I turned and ran forward, at the heart of our enemy. I charged Punch so suddenly and swiftly that even Judy stepped back, surprised. I ran straight at Punch, murder glinting in my eyes.

"Ha!" Punch laughed, and he raised his paddle and swung right at me.

I didn't block Punch's deadly swing. At the last moment, I turned aside, dashed left, and Punch's overhead axe-swing swished through the air, missing me by inches, and shattered the flagstones where I would've been. I dodged around him; he turned to face me, but I didn't strike at him. I whirled my jump rope and flicked it out with all of my might, gripping one handle as the other wooden handle flipped and flashed high, like the tip of a cracking bullwhip. The free handle swung fast and hard ... and forcefully hit the huge glass screen of the giant TV.

The giant TV exploded, showering glass shards across the whole hall in cloud of white smoke, and a rain of tiny, sharp fragments. The blast deafened us and shocked everyone.

Punch recovered first, unequaled fury in his eyes. He raised his paddle against me, but Judy hit Punch from behind; only that saved my life. I ran away as their fighting continued.

But the flying glamour dolls hovered frozen,

blinking stupidly, as if awakening from a groggy dream. Beneath their winged cousins, all of the glamour dolls staggered, shaking their heads, as if recovering from a dizzy mist.

"You're free!" I shouted at the glamour dolls. "Punch has been controlling you, convincing you that you needed things that you really don't, that you needed to maintain a beauty that you didn't have. You don't need make-up and fancy clothes! Your actions make you more beautiful, or more ugly, than any fashions ever could!"

The army of glamour dolls stood blinking, confused, staring at me as if seeing me for the first time. I stood before them, dressed like them, wearing the same make-up; Mr. Magee had said that the glamour dolls couldn't be defeated: this was my only hope. I needed them to see me as one of them, a fellow fashion model, even if only for a second. They stared bewildered, but then their penciled brows lowered and furrowed. Anger darkened their expressions, but not anger at me; they turned their hateful glares on Punch.

"No!" Punch cried, and he backed away from Judy as the glamour dolls advanced upon him, determined to exact their just retribution.

However, just as they approached, the swiftly-dimming light failed. The Factory darkened: the sun had set, casting The Factory in shadow.

"Yes!" Punch shouted triumphantly, and we all stopped, frozen in terror. With the sun beneath the

horizon, darkness covered the land, and upon the tall walls, infinitely-black shapes ascended: *the shadow puppets had arisen.*

"I've won!" Punch cried, his face twisted with evil glee. "Shadow puppets! Kill them! Smother them! Consume them all!"

Every fear in existence emanated from the shadow puppets, and I quailed before them. My Light-spell, I thought, but I was already exhausted; how long could I keep it up?

The magic is in the play!

"No!" I shouted at Punch. "Time for one more spell!"

I flipped up my jump rope, suddenly Speed-Jumping as fast as I could. With the last of my strength, I shouted one final chant.

"Great Aunt Virginia
Turn back time!
Young again!
Young again!
Youth be thine!"

As I chanted, Great Aunt Virginia's aged face paled and her expression grew horrified; *had I made another mistake, like I had when I'd forced my parents back together?* Would this plan of mine end just as ruinous as that one? *Had I just destroyed Arcadia with my childish foolishness?*

But I couldn't turn back now; the shadow puppets were closing in, The Factory growing darker, more fearful by the second. When their black outlines covered the last of the windows, then we'd be in total darkness, and they'd consume us with irresistible terrors. I flipped my rope faster and harder, chanting with all of my will. Great Aunt Virginia's eyes opened wide, and then her whole shape changed. Suddenly, where Great Aunt Virginia had stood, a young girl no more than nine years old stood in an old fashioned dress, just like in the ancient black-and-white photo that Great Aunt Virginia had shown me in her living room; *Great Aunt Virginia was young again.*

With the last of my strength, I flung my jump rope at her ... and then I collapsed onto the stone floor.

Young again, Great Aunt Virginia expertly caught the jump rope with all the dexterity and energy of youth, and an instant later, a glowing sphere enveloped her brighter than any I'd ever conjured. With a mastery that I'd never managed, Great Aunt Virginia jump-roped as she had all her life, with decades of practice that I hadn't had. She even threw in some of the tricks that she'd watched Hilary and I do.

Cries came from the shadow puppets as youthened Great Aunt Virginia's brilliant glow stabbed through them, and then her sphere of light expanded, suddenly, explosively, blasting out to fill the hall and stream through the very walls. Through the high windows, I saw her sphere of light blaze across the sky, expanding for miles in every direction, turning night into day. All of Arcadia glowed golden and silver, and even the clouds in the suddenly-brightened sky illuminated, revealing those sparkling linings seldom seen by mortal eyes.

With a final scream, the writhing shadow puppets succumbed to the light; they faded ... and were banished from Arcadia forever.

"No!" Punch screamed, and he drew back to hurl his paddle at Great Aunt Virginia, but Great Aunt Virginia released one handle and cracked her jump rope like a bullwhip, as I had; it snapped in the air, and a bolt of lightning thundered from its far handle, striking Punch electrically, making him thrash about uncontrollably. At the same instant, Judy smashed her paddle against his. Punch's grip faltered, failed, and then Punch's paddle clattered uselessly to the floor.

Judy continued her attack, and the unarmed Punch cried out in beaten agony. Under her relentless assault, Punch crawled to his feet, and ran away from Judy, straight at us, at me, as if he'd stomp me to death under his massive wooden boots. I screamed, but suddenly all of the glamour dolls charged forward, underfoot, seized his boots, tripped Punch, caught him as he fell atop them. Then, with strength powered by revenge, the angry glamour dolls hurled him into a stone wall. Punch cried out as he smashed into the hard stone wall, and then he crashed to the floor, helpless; Punch had no allies left.

Princess Gracely darted forward, raised her

graceful arms, and another giant rhinestone erupted, this one greater than before. Princess Gracely's crystal prison encased Punch from below his feet to just over his head. Punch was frozen, trapped inside the powerful crystalline rhinestone, helpless and impotent.

Punch was defeated!

"Yes!" Muskay cheered, and all of the dolls cheered with us. Turning around, I saw the baby dolls crowded in beside the glamour dolls, and behind them bunched rag dolls, marionettes, hand puppets, tin soldiers, nutcracker dolls, and even many of the neon-tufted troll dolls, all piled inside the doorway of The Factory, together cheering Punch's defeat.

Judy alone didn't smile, but looked upon her trapped husband, encased inside the giant rhinestone, with a mixture of disgust and sorrow; she was his wife. But Princess Gracely curtseyed deeply before her, and Judy bowed slightly in return.

"I'm so proud of you!" said a youthful voice, and I looked down upon Great Aunt Virginia, now three years younger than I, her smooth, shining face aglow with vitality and delight. She hugged me tightly, and I wrapped my arms fiercely around her and lifted her up; *Arcadia was free: we'd won.*

Suddenly, as I held her up high, Great Aunt Virginia grew unexpectedly heavy. Her slender limbs elongated, her tight skin loosened and wrinkled, and her feet stretched out to reach the ground and support her, despite that I was holding her over my head. Age had returned to Great Aunt Virginia, but the tightness with which she hugged me never faltered.

Amid the celebration, Hilary awoke, and Hiram set her gently onto her feet. She seemed dazed and exhausted, but slowly she grasped that we'd won as she spied Punch frozen, trapped inside of Princess Gracely's giant crystal rhinestone.

"We did it!" Hilary cheered. "We've won, and nothing can stop us now!"

"What do you mean?" I asked, and all around us, the cheering lessened, and every eye fell upon us.

"We triumphed ... and we have magic!" Hilary shouted. "We're going to be rich! Famous! We can have anything! Be anyone! We'll be the world's biggest celebrities, worshiped and adored! We'll have yachts and private jets, and reporters will beg to interview us. We'll be on TV! People will fawn over us night and day! We'll rule the world!"

"No," I said to Hilary. "We won because we played to win. Arcadia is just a game ..."

"But it doesn't have to be!" Hilary argued. "We can take it to the real world! We can do magic! We can do anything!"

"No, we can't," I said. "What about our friends, the dolls and animals ... and people of Arcadia?"

"We don't need them!" Hilary shouted, her exuberant face alight with triumph, almost resembling Punch. "We've got it all! We can conquer the world!"

"You sound serious," I said hesitantly.

"*I am!*" Hilary cried. "*We can have everything!*"

"That's too bad," I said to Hilary, truly sorry, but knowing that it had to be done. "I hope that you'll forgive me someday ... and that we can still be friends."

"What ...?" Hilary asked, confused.

"Reality," I said softly. "You've turned away from dolls and make-believe and accepted only our mother's world. *The magic is in the play:* you've banished yourself."

Slowly Hilary started to fade, to vanish, to shift back from Arcadia to home, back to Great Aunt Virginia's apartment, to be forever trapped there with both of our mothers.

"*Nooooo!!!!*" Hilary cried in anguish, and then she faded ... and she was gone.

As the remainder of the celebration was winding down, Princess Gracely took me outside, away from all the others, and we sat together upon the grass.

"I must tell you a story," Princess Gracely said. "Once upon a time, there were four beautiful girls ..."

"I know this story," I said. "Great Aunt Virginia told it to me, but there were only three beautiful girls ..."

"There were four girls when I told it to her," Princess Gracely said, and a distant sadness softened her voice. "Once upon a time, there were four beautiful girls.

"The first girl didn't believe in anything, not in magic

or dreams, and she had a very nice, plain, dull life.

"The second girl believed in many dreams, big and small, and some came true, but most didn't; the second girl reveled in her dreams come true, but spent most of her days bitter and resentful for her dreams that never came to be, and she suffered a most unhappy life.

"The third girl also believed in many dreams, big and small, and some came true, but most didn't; the third girl reveled in her dreams come true, and only thought fondly of her dreams that never came to be, grateful for the momentary joys that they had given her.

"The fourth girl believed only in her dreams that came true, and turned away from everything else that life had to offer; the fourth girl's life was as happy as the third girl's, but not as rich or fulfilling.

"The moral is: Never darken the dreams of a young-girl's heart, nor allow it to blind you to the joys of becoming a woman; to be truly happy, you must have both."

I stared at Princess Gracely, not wanting to discuss this.

"G-Great Aunt V-Virginia ... is the ... f-fourth g-girl, isn't she?" I asked.

"Yes," Princess Gracely said. "Great Aunt Virginia has enjoyed a wonderful life here, but she never married, and never had children of her own; never had a life outside of her dreams. You are our new jumper; you'll always be welcomed here, but you don't have to live in only one world; you can have both: *you don't have to give up on your dreams to have a real life."*

Weeks later, I was seated by Madame Paprus in the place of honor, front-row-center, with Great Aunt Virginia on one side of me, Muskay beside her, Princess Gracely on the other side, and Hiram beside her. In the back, watching over everyone else, stood Judy, Falcon, my Pegasus, and my Purple Dragon, all smiling and enjoying the show. Upon the two-hundred red velvet chairs in The Palace, now fully-restored by the hand puppets and spotlessly-cleaned by the rag dolls, all of the dolls in Arcadia were gathered, all mixed together, trolls and paper dolls, glamour dolls, rag dolls, baby dolls, tin soldiers, nutcrackers, and hand puppets, all carefully restored and mended after the ravages of battle, and many laughing stuffed animals filled the aisles.

Upon the stage, Mr. Magee tap-danced with amazing agility, while all of the marionettes clomped loudly behind him, and every doll with a musical instrument played a spritely melody, while a chorus of glamour dolls sang. All of the dolls clapped and cheered together, and the marionettes finished with a great flourish, and Mr. Magee tossed his cane into the air, and it burst into a bouquet of flowers, baby roses, and I cheered along with the rest. Arcadia was free, peaceful, and better than ever, and I was its magical guardian, and

I would never fail in my duty ... or forget the importance of play ... or the importance of living.

THE END

JUMP ROPE JUMPS

Basic Skills

- Basic Double Bounce

1. All you do is simply jump twice in one rotation of the rope.

- Basic Single Bounce

1. Just jump once over the rope instead of jumping twice.

- Single Sideswing

1. Put your hands together, while holding the handles, and swing the rope from one side of your body to the other.
2. Keep repeating step 1.
3. When you are ready, open your hands. Swing the rope down and jump.

- Skier

1. Jump side to side like you're skiing.

- Side Straddle

1. Pretend you're doing a jumping jack using only your feet.

- Front Straddle

1. Jump with one foot in front and the other in back.
2. Jump and switch the positions of your feet.

- X-to-Straddle

1. Jump with your feet spread apart.
2. Jump and cross your legs.

3. Repeat steps 1 and 2.

- Heel Exchange

1. Jump and touch your heel to the ground in front of you.

2. Switch feet and touch the other heel to the ground in front of you.

3. Keep repeating steps 1 and 2.

- Toe Exchange

1. Jump and touch your toe to the ground behind you.

2. Switch feet and touch the other toe to the ground behind you.

3. Keep repeating steps 1 and 2.

- Jogging Steps

1. Turn the rope and step over the rope with one foot.

2. On the next turn of the rope step over the rope with the other foot.

3. Keep repeating steps 1 and 2.

Intermediate Skills

- Irish Fling

1. This is an 8 step skill.

2. With the first turn of the rope land on one foot and tap the other foot out to the side.

3. With the second turn of the rope land on the same foot and tap the other foot out in front of your body but slightly out to the side.

4. With the third turn of the rope land on the same foot and tap the other foot out in front of your body.

5. With the fourth turn of the rope land on the same foot and bend the other leg so your ankle is in front of your knee.

6. The next four steps you do the same thing on the other side.

- Front Cross

1. With the first turn of the rope jump a regular jump.
2. With the second turn of the rope cross your arms and jump through the loop that you made with the rope.

- Wounded Duck

1. Jump up in the air and land with your toes pointing in.
2. Jump up and land with your toes pointing out.
3. Keep repeating this.

- Front Kicks

1. With the first turn of the rope land on both feet.
2. With the second turn of the rope land on your left foot and kick your right.
3. With the third turn of the rope land on both feet.
4. With the fourth turn of the rope land on your right foot and kick your left.

- Double Under

1. Start with a single bounce.
2. Jump high into the air and turn the rope as fast as you can.
3. If you do this right the rope should pass under you twice before you land.

- Leg-Over

1. Jump a single bounce.
2. Pull your right leg up and jump the rope with your left leg, while putting your right arm under your right knee.

3. Now pull your arm out from under your leg and do a sideswing.

• Leg-Over Cross

This trick is the same as the leg over but instead of putting your right arm under your right leg, you cross your arms and put your left arm under your right leg.

Advanced Skills

• Cross Cross

1. Start like you do with the cross.
2. When you cross you must quickly uncross and cross again before you jump the rope.
3. Your arms should have crossed twice in one jump, if not, keep trying.

• Front Back Cross

1. Do a single bounce and then do a sideswing.
2. Keep one arm crossing the front of your body and one arm crossing behind your back.
3. Jump through the rope and then go back into a sideswing.

• Between Knees Cross

1. Bend over and put your arms between your knees and cross them.
2. When the rope comes down, jump it.
3. When you pull your arms out, the rope should start going backwards.

• Behind the Knees Cross

1. Bend over and cross your arms behind your knees.
2. Jump the rope and uncross your arms.

- Behind the Back Cross

1. Start with a single bounce.
2. When you cross, cross with both arms behind your back.
3. Jump the rope and quickly uncross your arms.
4. Your arms should have gone behind your back while you jumped the rope.

- Push-ups

1. Start with a single bounce.
2. Jump low to the ground.
3. Put your hands on the ground and extend your legs so you are in a push-up position. The rope should not be moving at this point.
4. Jump up and pull the rope under your feet.

- Rump Jump

For this, you just sit down with your legs out in front of your body and try to bounce while swinging the rope from the side underneath you as you bounce on your rump.

- Behind the Back/ Behind the Knees Cross

1. Bend over and put your left hand behind your knees and your right hand behind your back.
2. Your arms should be as if they were crossed.
3. Jump the rope and pull your arms out back to your side.

- Speed Rope

1. Jump as fast as you can swing the rope – the fastest wins!

ABOUT THE AUTHOR

Born in Tripler Army Medical Center, Honolulu, Hawaii, Jay Palmer works as a technical writer in the software industry in Seattle, Washington. Jay enjoys parties, reading everything in sight, woodworking, obscure board games, and riding his Kawasaki Vulcan. Jay is a knight in the SCA, frequently attends writer conferences, SciFi Conventions, and he and Karen are both avid ballroom dancers. But most of all, Jay enjoys writing.